Phœnicia and Israel. a Historical Essay

PHŒNICIA AND ISRAEL.

A Historical Essay.

BY

AUGUSTUS S. WILKINS, M.A.,

**FELLOW OF UNIVERSITY COLLEGE, LONDON;
LATE SCHOLAR OF ST. JOHN'S COLLEGE, CAMBRIDGE;
PROFESSOR OF LATIN IN OWENS COLLEGE, MANCHESTER.**

πολυμερῶς καὶ πολυτρόπως.

LONDON :

HODDER AND STOUGHTON,

27, PATERNOSTER ROW.

MDCCCLXXI.

THIS ESSAY OBTAINED THE BURNEY PRIZE
IN THE UNIVERSITY OF CAMBRIDGE FOR
THE YEAR 1870.

The late RICHARD BURNEY, ESQ., M.A., of
Christ's College, Cambridge, previously to his
death on the 30th November, 1845, empow-
ered his Cousin, Mr. Archdeacon Burney, to
offer, through the Vice-Chancellor, to the University of Cambridge, the sum of £3,500 Reduced Three per Cent. Stock, for the purpose of
establishing an Annual Prize, to be awarded to
the Graduate who should produce the best
Essay on a subject to be set by the Vice-
Chancellor.

On the day after this offer was communicated
to the Vice-Chancellor, Mr. Burney died ; but
his sister and executrix, Miss J. Caroline Burney, being desirous of carrying her brother's
intentions into effect, generously renewed the
offer.

The Prize is to be awarded to a Graduate of
the University, who is not of more than three
years' standing from admission to his first
degree when the Essays are sent in, and who

shall produce the best English Essay " on some moral or metaphysical subject, on the Existence, Nature, and Attributes of God, or on the Truth and Evidence of the Christian Religion." The successful Candidate is required to print his Essay ; and after having delivered, or caused to be delivered, a copy of it to the University Library, the Library of Christ's College, the University Libraries of Oxford, Dublin, and Edinburgh, and to each of the Adjudicators of the Prize, he is to receive from the Vice-Chancellor the year's interest of the Stock, from which sum the Candidate is to pay the expenses of printing the Essay.

The Vice-Chancellor, the Master of Christ's College, and the Norrisian Professor of Divinity, are the Examiners of the Compositions and the Adjudicators of the Prize.

In the event of the exercises of two of the Candidates being deemed by the Examiners to possess equal merit, if one of such Candidates be a member of Christ's College, the Prize is to be adjudged to him.

The subject proposed by the Vice-Chancellor for the year 1870 was—*The Influence of the Phœnicians on the Political, Social, and Religious Relations of the Children of Israel.*

PREFACE.

THE following Essay cannot pretend to be a
complete discussion of the subject of which it
treats. This is so vast, and in many points so
obscure, involving as it does many of the most
perplexed and disputed questions of ancient
history, culture, mythology, and religion, that
it might furnish a worthy theme for scholars of
the most extensive learning and the greatest
intuitive sagacity. And the present volume
appears under special disadvantages. Written
in the midst of other pressing duties, where no
good library of modern theological works was
available for reference, and composed very
hurriedly under the restrictions as to time im-
posed by the conditions of a University competition, it is now printed, in accordance with the
University regulations, precisely as it was submitted to the adjudicators, with the exception of
verbal corrections and a few additional references.

But there are two considerations which diminish the reluctance with which I allow this Essay to appear. I believe it is the only work of the kind in English (and as far as I know in French or German) which aims directly at gathering in a focus the scattered rays of light that we have from many quarters upon one of the most powerful influences that tended to mould the character of the Chosen People. And I think that, though many authorities, which I should have been glad to consult, were inaccessible under the circumstances in which the Essay was written, those that have been employed have been the most complete and trustworthy. M. Rénan's " Histoire des Langues Semitiques" appears to leave little to be desired in its own department. And the great work of Movers, without whose constant aid I should never have attempted this subject, is a complete repertory of all that up to the date of its publication (1841—1856) had been learnt about Phœnicia. The following pages would not, I hope, be without their value, if they only rendered more accessible to students of history and theology the main results to which his vast erudition and unwearied industry have led him. To supplement his researches, I have had recourse in many places to the works of Professor Rawlinson and M. Lenormant, but not

without a certain amount of distrust, felt often
when it has not been expressed. It would be
of course ridiculous to depreciate the value of
the recent attempts to decipher the cuneiform inscriptions. But those scholars who have under-
taken to weave the fragmentary Assyrian records
into a consecutive history seem to have lost
sight far too often of the golden canon of the
historian :—

νᾶφε καὶ μέμνασ' ἀπιστεῖν · ἄρθρα ταῦτα τᾶν φρενῶν.

In their eagerness to leave nothing unex-
plained, nothing uncertain, they appear sometimes to be building on the slightest foundations.
It is easy to understand the temptation to substitute assertion for suggestion ; but when one
or two palpable instances of the operation of
this tendency have been discovered, a serious
blow is inflicted on the confidence of the
reader. Fortunately, the guidance of such
authorities is needed mainly on points less
immediately connected with the present subject ; and their theories, however uncertified, are
not likely to lead us far wrong in our principal
conclusions.

A word or two may be added as to the
interest of the questions discussed in this Essay.
I should be sorry to subscribe to the doctrine

of a distinguished Professor, that the study of
history is mainly valuable as casting light upon
the political problems of the present day. I do
not suppose ·that Cicero was thinking only of
the needs of a statesman when he wrote, " Nes-
cire quid antea quam natus sis acciderit; id est
semper esse puerum." If we are to have a
scientific study of history, that study must be
pursued, as the study of any other branch of
knowledge, purely from a love of truth, unac-
companied by any merely utilitarian considerations ; for thus alone can we be preserved from
wresting the facts to suit our preconceived ideas,
and from searching for what we fancy should be,
rather than for that which is the truth.

> Oh, if we draw a circle premature
> Heedless of far gain,
> Greedy for quick returns of profit, sure
> Bad is our bargain !

Let us rather, like the patient scholars of old,

> Earn the means first—God surely will contrive
> Use for our earning.

But one lesson seems to lie on the surface of
such a discussion as the present. Many people
are distressed and alarmed at the growing tendency to assimilate the history of the Jews to
that of other ancient nations ; to eliminate the

miraculous, wherever it is possible to do so ; and
to regard the earlier portions of their annals as
largely imbued with the mythical element. This
is not the place to discuss how far this tendency
is in the direction of juster views. But may it
not be largely for good, if it leads us to dwell
rather upon the points in which the Jews re-
sembled other nations, than upon those on which
they differed from them? Do we not gain
rather than lose by considering Israel as a typical instead of an exceptional people? Miracles
are often spoken of as violations of the order of
nature : they are far rather revelations of the
true order of nature—glimpses given us for a
moment of the living Power that is working for
our blessing under the guise of a regular se-
quence of phenomena, but independent of and
far transcending all phenomenal manifestation.
And as the feeding of the five thousand lifts
for us the veil that hangs over the daily feeding
of the thousand millions of living men, so the
inspired record of the training of Israel for the
advent of the Lord is merely the key to the
right apprehension of the training of Rome, of
Greece, and of Germany, for the part they
should have in the Church of Christ. And if
we hold fast to this central truth of history, as
revealed to us first in the Hebrew prophets, and

afterwards expanded to its full proportions in the teaching of St. Paul, it will matter to us little if the researches of modern criticism shall show us that the living faith of the former in the Divine teaching and guidance was mixed with something of error as to its extent and the modes of its manifestation. The Old Testament becomes to us not less, but rather much more precious when we find its records revealing to us, not an isolated instance of favouritism, but a typical instance of the training of all the families of men for the coming of the Light and. Life of the world. The aim of this Essay will be fully reached if it should be found to help any to see, from a fragment of one of its strands, something of the beauty of the golden cord that binds into one great whole the changeful history of the tribes of man.

CONTENTS.

PHŒNICIA AND ISRAEL.

CHAPTER I.

INTRODUCTION.

Aryan and Semitic Migrations—Early Semitic Population of Canaan—Language substantially the same as Hebrew—Character of the Population—The Descent into Egypt—Its Date.

THE earliest glimpses that we are able to gain of primitive history, show us the two great stocks from which the civilization of the world has proceeded, in process of migration from their original abodes. From the uplands of central Asia, to which all converging testimony[1] seems to point, as the home of the Aryan race, the streams that were to fertilize

1 Gathered well by Pictet : " Les Aryas Primitifs," vol. i., Paris, 1859 ; and by A. Kuhn in Weber's " Indische Studien," vol. i.

the regions of Europe and of Indo-Persian Asia,
seem to have taken their rise. The former
poured on its western, way, throwing off as it
went the branches which developed into the
Sclavonic, the Teutonic, the Greek, and the
Italian peoples; and finally bore the Keltic
tribes to the utmost limits of the West. The
latter, diverging, after some indefinite lapse of
time from the early days when the stream that
was the first to leave its home had been severed
from it, took its course partly to the south-west,
to people the land of Iran, partly to the south-
east, to the country of the five rivers, thence in
long years to spread over the whole of the penin-
sula of India. Or perhaps the metaphor would
be more true if, instead of diverging streams, we
spoke of successive waves following each other
at distant intervals, but with all the various
sections of the European Aryans, ever pursuing
a westward course.[1] In this case philology is
hardly able as yet to decide between the two
expressions. But in the case of the Semitic

[1] Schleicher's Compendium, p. 11. This philologer,
however, differs from most other good authorities by
making the Slavo-German family break off from the main .
body before the separation into Eastern and Western
peoples, or Aryas and Yawanas.

peoples, there can be little doubt which is the more correct. We find no traces there of a movement, embracing at first the whole, or even one great section, of the original stock, and breaking off into various directions as isolated bodies severed themselves from the general mass. The most competent authorities teach us rather to conceive of successive waves of population, issuing from the mountainous country near the sources of the Euphrates and the Tigris, to which the narrative of Genesis points as the cradle of the human race, and to which the Mosaic accounts of the Deluge bring us back as the centre from which the children of Noah went forth again to people the earth. Of all the migrations from the land of Kir (Amos ix. 7) to the regions that lay south-west of it, that which is of the greatest importance in the history of man is undoubtedly the one with which the Bible connects the name of Terah. But this was so far from being the first of the movements in this direction, that it is much more likely to have been the last.[1] The anthropomorphic language of the Mosaic record is certainly not intended to hinder us from the quest of secondary

[1] Rénan, "Histoire des Langues Semitiques," p. 28.

causes for the change of abode, which it ascribes
to the direct command of the Deity. It was
probably partly in consequence of the barren-
ness of the upper valley of the Euphrates, that
rendered it little fitted for the home of a pastoral
tribe;[1] partly from the establishment of a powerful
non-Semitic empire upon the banks of the Tigris,[2]
leading, according to an old tradition, which may
be accepted in its general meaning, even if its
details bear the stamp of later invention, to the
persecution of those who clung to the purer faith,
that the family of Abraham found its way into
the more fertile and peaceful land of Canaan.[3]
But the same causes which had urged him on, we
may believe to have been powerful with kindred
tribes. Other branches of the Semitic stock,
with the incapacity for military organization
which seems inherent in these nomadic children
of the desert, would have found themselves unable to withstand the overwhelming numbers
that obeyed the commands of the Cushite
despots. And it may be that, whatever the

[1] Lenormant, "Ancient History" (E. T.), i., p. 80.
[2] Rénan, p. 33.
[3] Joseph. Ant., 1, 7, 1. Cp. Stanley, "Jewish Church,"
i., p. 17.

moral and religious degradation into which they
afterwards fell, they still retained enough of
this primitive monotheism, to induce them to
shrink with horror from the gross idolatry of the
barbarous hordes to whose power they were
compelled to yield. Be this as it may, all evidence that we have confirms the supposition
that long before the days of Abraham, Semitic
tribes had pressed along the path by which the
Divine guidance was to lead him, to the land
that should afterwards be possessed by his descendants, as the sand that is by the sea-shore
for multitude.

Of these preceding tribes some had pushed on
beyond the limits of the Promised Land, into
the yet more fertile valley of the Nile. The
best recent authorities [1] teach us to see in the
Hyksos, who have furnished so much matter for
debate to historians, "a wave of Semitic nomads,
who disturbed for a time Egyptian civilization,
and finally yielded to the resistance which an
organized society always successfully opposes to
undisciplined force." [2] But many remained in

[1] Movers, i. 32 ; Rénan, p. 38, and the authorities there
quoted ; Ewald, i., pp. 389, 399. (E. T.)
[2] Rénan, p. 38.

the land of Canaan, waging apparently ceaseless
war with the aboriginal tribes, the Rephaim, the
Zamzummim,[1] the Emim, and the Anakim, but
never meeting with entire success until the work
was taken in hand by the children of Israel,
hardened by the discipline of the desert, and
strong with the belief in a Divine "Captain of
the Armies of the Lord."

According to this account, Abraham, on his
first arrival in the Land of Promise, found the
population consisting, at least in a very large
measure, of tribes with which he would have
close affinities of blood and language.[2] This
seems, at first sight, utterly at variance with the
common conception of him as a solitary wan-
dering stranger in the midst of strangers.[3] And
yet the evidence would appear to bear it out.
For in the first place we have not the least hint

---

[1] Rénan seems to be right in considering this an onoma-
topoetic name for an "unintelligibly-speaking people," like
the βάρβαροι of the Greeks, the *mlechha* of the Sanskrit-
speaking Aryans. Cp. M. Müller: Lectures, i., p. 83,
with note.

[2] Ewald, i., p. 231.

[3] Herder (Geist der Ebräischen Poesie, p. 318, 1st ed.,
Dial. x.) finds this so incredible that he asserts that the
Phœnicians usurped the language of the Jews, probably
for the sake of commerce.

in' the Biblical narrative that points to any difference of language, such as we often have when the Jews came into contact with nations whose speech was really unintelligible to them ; as, for instance, the Egyptians (Psalm lxxxi. 5, cxiv. 1), the Assyrians (Isa. xxxvi. 11), and the Chaldees (Jer. v. 15). On the contrary, we find Abraham negotiating with the children of Heth, Isaac making a treaty with Abimelech, king of Gerar, Jacob and his sons "communing" with the people of Shechem, without the slightest reference to the need of any interpreter between them. Again, the names of persons and places in the early days when Abraham first visited the land, we find to have been such as admit at once of explanation from the Hebrew or the Phœnician language. "Melchizedek" is "the King of Righteousness;" "Abimelech," "the Father of the King ;" "Kirjath-sepher," "the City of the Book," and so on. A suggestion has indeed been made that these are only Hebrew translations of the original forms; but this is sufficiently disproved by the analogy of similar cases, where we find no such translation to have taken place. It is indeed most unlikely that, if the nations of Canaan had spoken a dialect

essentially different from that of the Hebrews,
the latter should have ever understood sufficiently the meaning of the proper names in use
among their neighbours, to have translated them
into names of corresponding signification among
themselves. But the most convincing proof lies
in the fact of the clearly demonstrated identity
of race between the Canaanites and the·Phœni-
cians. The Biblical account in Gen. x., which
makes Sidon the first-born of Canaan, is abundantly confirmed by independent evidence. The
Septuagint frequently renders Canaan and Canaanite in the Hebrew by Phœnicia and Phœnician.[1] S. Augustine tells us that the Carthaginian
Phœnicians still retained the name : for " inter-
rogati rustici nostri quid sint, Punice respon-
dentes, Canani, corrupta scilicet sicut in talibus
una littera (accurate enim dicere debebant Cha-
nani) quid aliud respondent quam Chananæi ? "[2]
The Phœnicians seem to have known their land
by no other name than *Chna*, "the low-lying ";[3]
and one of the coins of Laodicea still extant,

---

[1] Kenrick, p. 42, note 3.
[2] *Epist. ad Rom.*, § 12, quoted very incompletely by
Kenrick, p. 42.
[3] Movers, ii., p. 6.

bears the inscription "a mother in Canaan."[1]
Movers has indeed succeeded in showing that the
people known to the Hebrews under the name
of Canaanites did not form one united nation,
sharply distinguished from the surrounding
tribes; that the appellation had originally a
geographical rather than an ethnological meaning; and that the district over which it extended
was peopled rather by successive immigrations
than by one united invasion.[2] Still, all this does
not shake the conclusion, to which we are
brought by very much evidence, that there was
such a similarity in language between the Phœnicians and the rest of the inhabitants of the
Promised Land, as to cause the Israelites to
apply to the latter generally, a name which
belonged primarily and especially to the former.
Now, as we shall have occasion to notice at
more length further on, there cannot be the
least doubt as to the close connection between
the Phœnician language and Hebrew. They belong, not only to the same family of languages,
but also to the same subdivision of it. The
testimony of two of the Fathers, S. Jerome,

[1] Movers, ii., pp. 11 (with note 36) and 120.
[2] ii., pp. 62—82.

himself a learned Hebrew scholar, and S. Augustine, born in a Punic-speaking district, is confirmed by the researches of later scholars; and
Hebrew is found to supply the key to the Punic
passage in the Pœnulus of Plautus,[1] to the
etymology of the Phœnician and Carthaginian
names preserved to us, and to the Phœnician
inscriptions that have been gathered with care,
and interpreted with vast learning and brilliant
intuitive skill by Gesenius[2] and Movers. The
former scholar expresses his judgment on the
language of Phœnicia in the following decided
and decisive terms: "Omnino hoc tenendum
est, pleraque et pæne omnia cum Hebræis con-
venire, sive radices spectas, sive verborum et
formandorum et flectendorum rationem."[3]

The demonstration of this substantial identity
between the language of Canaan and Hebrew,
"obviously leads," in the opinion of Mr. Twisleton, "to the conclusion that the Hebrews *adopted*

[1] Best interpreted by Movers, Phön. Texte: Erster
Theil, 1845.

[2] "Scripturæ Linguæque Phœniciæ Monumenta,"
Leipzig, 1837.

[3] Mon. Phœn., p. 335 (quoted in Dict. of Bible). Of
ninety-four words in the important Marseilles inscription,
seventy-four occur in the Old Testament.

Phœnician as their own language ;"[1] and Mr.
Kenrick says, still more positively, "The progenitors of the Jews must have spoken Syriac
(*i.e.*, Aramæan), not Hebrew, that is, Canaanitic."[2]
But against this supposition, maintained by some
of the older critics, there are several considerations which ought to weigh with us. In
the first place, nations, especially in primitive
times when difference of dialect was a greater
barrier than even now, are rarely found to
change their language, except for one of the
three following causes : it may be from conquest, as was the case of the Gauls when they
learnt the tongue of their Roman masters ; it
may be from the attractions of a higher civilization, as with the Normans when they adopted
French ; it may be the result of close social
intercourse, of intermarriages, and of the neces-
sities of trade, as with the German immigrants
into the United States of America. But none
of these causes are found in the case which we
are now discussing. Abraham was never in
subjection to any of the surrounding tribes ;.
whatever may have been the case at the time of

---

[1] Dict. Bible, ii., p. 863*b*.
[2] Phœnicia, p. 49 ; Rénan, p. 111.

the invasion of Joshua, they do not seem to have
attained in his days any height of civilization
superior to his own simple pastoral life; and
this prototype of the Bedouin sheik, with his
herds and flocks, and his three hundred and
eighteen trained men born in his own house,
lived a free, self-sufficing life, in friendly but
apparently in slight relations with the neighbouring chieftains. What possible inducement
could there have been for him to abandon the
language, endeared by memories of worship in
his early and distant home, and to adopt that of
the people around, with whom he had so little
intercourse? And the probability of such a step
decreases with every expansion of the original
tribe-like household. It is much more natural
to suppose, with M. Rénan,[1] that Hebrew, such
as we have it now in the Sacred Volume, was
developed in the course of the prolonged and
intimate contact of two nations speaking dialects
closely resembling each other, to begin with.
But this once established, we may reasonably
allow that of the two the language of the children

---

[1] p. 112, who refers to Bertheau—" Zur Geschichte der
Israeliten," p. 179. "Phœnician may be called a tissue, in
which Hebrew forms the woof, and Syrian [Aramaic] the
warp." Bunsen, Philosophy of Universal History, i., p. 244.

of Israel approached the more nearly to the Aramæan, such as it was afterwards spoken in the region from which Abraham came, and that it contributed important Aramaic elements to the later Biblical Hebrew.[1]

We are thus brought back to the conclusion, already stated, that when Abraham was brought by the guidance of God into the land of Canaan, he found himself in the midst of a population which could not be regarded as wholly alien. Nor do the inhabitants appear to have been of a character which would repel all intercourse. They had already abandoned, at least to a certain extent, their original pastoral and nomadic habits, and we find them gathered together into cities, leaving the open country principally to the occupation of friendly strangers, such as Abraham. But their civilization was but little developed ; for good and for evil, they seem to

---

[1] According to Mr. Kenrick (Phœnicia, p. 167, note 3), "Movers (Ersch and Gruber, Encycl. Art. Phönizien) has collected with great care the differences between the Phœnician and the Bible Hebrew, and finds that the former leans much to Aramæan forms." But this is to be explained by the fact that the specimens of Phœnician preserved to us are of a later date than the Hebrew. Both languages seem to have passed through the same Aramaising process. (Cp. Rénan, Histoire, p. 189.)

have retained much of their primitive character.
Where kings are mentioned, they approach more
nearly to the patriarchal heads of tribes than to
the barbarous despots of later days. We come
across no traces of the fearful moral corruption
that afterwards made "the land spue out" its
inhabitants, except, indeed, in the wealthy and
luxurious Cities of the Plain. There the degene-
racy that was afterwards to bring the Divine
judgments upon all the nations of Canaan, had
rapidly run its fatal course. But the rest of the
land was still comparatively uncorrupted; in
the story of Dinah, the conduct of Shechem and
Hamor displays a willingness to atone for the
effects of overmastering passion, that contrasts
very favourably with the treachery of the sons
of Jacob ; the tone of the court of Gerar, in the
intercourse of the king with Abraham and with
Isaac, appears to us singularly high ; and the
language of Ephron the Hittite is full of the
most graceful Oriental courtesy. But the scene
which most reveals to us the purity of religion
and morality which still remained, is that in
which the Father of the Faithful met the
mysterious figure who was "first by interpretation king of righteousness, and after that king .

of Salem, which is king of peace." Whatever spiritual or typical meaning we may consider ourselves authorized to draw from the narrative, its primary significance undoubtedly is, that in the midst of the ever-increasing darkness there was one at least whom Abraham acknowledged as the priest of the Most High God. And even one such centre of light cannot have been without its influences in staying the advent of the gloom that was soon to cover the nations.

With the journey of Jacob and all his household to join his sons in Egypt, the scene of the sacred narrative is removed from Canaan; and when, following the journeyings of the chosen people, we are brought back again to its confines, the change that has passed over the country is indeed surprising. But as this seems partly at least to have arisen from the action of foreign nations, it is needful that we should first turn our glance upon these for a moment.

Our subject, fortunately, does not require us to plunge into the complications of Egyptian and early Jewish chronology. Numerous and widely differing attempts have been made to fit the one into the other, but a just caution will lead us to follow the example of the late Dean

Milman (*quem honoris causa nomino*) in refusing entire assent to any.[1] Still numerous slight indications warrant the conjecture that the Pharaoh with whom Abraham was brought in such friendly relations belonged to the dynasty of the Shepherd Kings. The absence of any reference to an interpreter, the simple Theism implied in the recorded expressions of the king, and the hearty and courteous welcome given to the powerful chief of the nomad tribe, which seems to have been closely connected by blood and language with the conquering Hyksos invaders, all lead us to the same conclusion.[2]

When we come to consider the second descent into Egypt under Jacob, the condition of affairs is greatly changed. The imperial splendours of the court, the power of the native priesthood, (always repressed and discountenanced under the alien dynasty), the suspicion and dread of strangers, especially of such as belong to a nomad pastoral tribe, the un-Semitic character of the names recorded (as demonstrated by Lepsius), all combine to prove that the intruders

[1] "History of the Jews," i., p. 102. See especially the very striking passage from Bredow quoted in the prefatory note to Book vi. (p. 237, last ed.)

[2] Cp. Ewald, i., pp. 392—400.

had been by now expelled, and that the successors to the ancient monarchs had regained the throne. On the other hand, it seems pretty certain that during the life of Joseph, Egypt had not yet entered on that warlike policy of aggression and conquest that carried the victorious arms of Sethos and of Rameses over so large a portion of Western Asia. We shall therefore be probably right in assigning the entrance of the children of Israel into the land of Goshen to some point within the period that elapsed between the expulsion of the Hyksos dynasty, and the accession of the conquering nineteenth dynasty. If this be correct, the relations of Canaan to Egypt will come out clearly. During the greater portion of the time in which the patriarchs were still in the Promised Land, a friendly but independent alliance would seem to have existed between them, changed towards the end by the expulsion of the Shepherd Kings into a feeling of strong aversion, which sometimes even broke out into open hostilities. M. Lenormant[1] has brought evidence for believing that probably with the approval and even the assistance of the reigning eighteenth dynasty,

[1] i., p. 92.

the children of Israel had made several attempts
to win for themselves the land promised to their
fathers. " Thus mention is made of an expedition of the sons of Ephraim against the people
of Gath, whose cattle they drove off, but who
slew them (1 Chron. vii. 21). A daughter of
Ephraim built several cities in the land of
Canaan (1 Chron. vii. 24). Lastly, it is mentioned that the family of Shelah, son of Judah,
had made conquests in the territory of Moab
(1 Chron. iv. 21, 22)."

This is only part of the general policy, the
results of which are depicted on the contemporary monuments of Egypt. There we find
the Egyptian forces constantly engaged in the
reduction of the little forts of the petty kings
of Palestine.[1] But rulers like Amenophis and
Thothmes the First and the Third do not seem
to have cared to subdue the country entirely ;
they were satisfied with exacting an acknowledgment of supremacy, the payment of tribute
and military service. The main struggle appears
to have been with the Khita, or Hittites,—not
that comparatively insignificant tribe whose
capital was Kirjath-Arba, but a much more

[1] i., p. 228.

powerful northern branch, which extended north
of Palestine from the Euphrates to the sea.
We cannot doubt that the heavy blows inflicted
on this Canaanitish empire by the conquering
kings of the eighteenth dynasty, and still more
by the monarchs who succeeded it, proved of
essential service in lightening the task that
afterwards lay before the army of Joshua. An
Egyptian poet of the time puts·these exalted
words into the mouth of Amen, the Theban
sun-god :—

I am come—to thee have I given to strike down Syrian
 princes.
Under thy feet they lie throughout the breadth of the
 country.
Like to the Lord of light, I made them see thy glory,
Blinding their eyes with light, the earthly image of Amen.

The accession of a king "who knew not
Joseph" apparently denotes not only a change
of dynasty, but also a change of policy. The
measures of Joseph seem to have been directed
mainly to the development of the resources of
the country, especially by the encouragement of
agriculture in the fertile expanse of Lower Egypt.
But if we are right in assigning his viceroyalty
to the time of one or other of the two great
kings that bore the name of Thothmes, Dean

Milman can hardly be correct in speaking of
the policy of this reign as pacific,[1] and contrasted sharply with the splendid Rameseid
period of war. There is no reign of this epoch
whose monumental records do not supply us
with long lists of conquered tribes and nations.
He is more happy in the stress he lays upon
the increasing importance of Thebes under the
nineteenth dynasty, as denoting a diminished
concern for the peaceful development of agriculture. But the cause of the change of policy
he does not dwell upon: M. Lenormant has
advanced a theory of it, which seems to be more
than an ingenious conjecture.[2] The close of
the eighteenth dynasty was marked by great
religious disturbances : Amenhotep IV., a prince
whose physiognomy differs strangely from that
of the other Egyptian kings, made a determined
attempt to change the religion of the country,
and to establish in the place of the polytheism
hitherto universal, the worship of a single god—
Aten—represented under the form of the sun's
disc, and possibly identical with the Hebrew
Adonai. Is it inconceivable that the children of
Israel, now wonderfully increased in numbers,

[1] i., p. 112.   [2] i., p. 238.

and led perhaps by some one who had an influence at the court of the Pharaoh similar to that afterwards won by Daniel, Mordecai, and Nehemiah at the court of Persia, should have contributed largely to this imperfect monotheism? The monumental evidence of Tell-el-Amarm, the new capital of Amenhotep, tends to confirm this supposition. The chronology exactly coincides, on the hypothesis which we have adopted throughout. And when the disorders were at last suppressed, and a new and vigorous dynasty established, what could be more natural than a fierce persecution directed against the nation which had shown itself strong enough already to shake to the foundation the beliefs and the worship of the country? To the bitterness of religious animosity, the jealousy of national antipathy was shortly added. The Egyptian dominion in Syria was seriously threatened by the great confederacy of the Khitas, now formed into a single monarchy; the Canaanites of Palestine were naturally attracted to them by community of race, and were eager to throw off all dependence upon Egypt; the children of Israel were probably, as we have seen above, closely connected with the Canaan-

ites ; and nothing is more natural to suppose
than that this connection should have greatly
increased the suspicion with which they were
regarded by the Egyptians.   We can readily believe that Rameses II., during the severe struggle
which was needed, as we know from the monuments, before he could make any sort of peace
with this powerful people, exercised all manner
of severities upon the Hebrews in the land of
Goshen, with the very purpose, ascribed to him
in the Bible, " lest they multiply, and it came to
pass, that when there falleth out any war, they
join also unto our enemies, and fight against us."
The struggle in the north of Canaan, with very
important effects to be afterwards discussed,
which had filled so large a portion of the reign
of Seti, was terminated by a peace, upon something like equal terms, early in the reign of
Rameses, and the fifty years of quiet that
followed were occupied with the extensive building which proved such a burden to the children
of Israel. " In all the monuments of Rameses,
there is hardly a stone, so to speak, which has
not cost a human life.[1]   The calm judgment of
history confirms the stigma fixed on him by the

[1] Lenormant, i., p. 257.

Bible." "And it came to pass in process of
time that the king of Egypt died: and the
children of Israel sighed by reason of the bondage, and they cried, and their cry came up unto
God by reason of the bondage." The nineteenth
dynasty marks the Augustan age of Egypt;[1]
but it closes in gloom and darkness. "Not only
have the stately structures ceased to arise, the
expanding walls to be decorated with processions
of tribute-bearing kings and nations, but there
is a significant silence in the existing monuments: the names and titles of their kings, in
their characteristic cartouches, are no longer
lavishly inscribed upon them; but there are
signs of erasure, of studious concealment, as of
something which they would shrink from committing to imperishable memory. Some disaster
seems to have fallen upon the realm, which
rather than commemorate, the records break off
and are mute."[2] The solution of this mystery is
furnished only by the Mosaic narrative. Mi-
renptah or Amenophis, the son of the great
oppressor, had hardened his heart, and refused
to let the children of Israel be led forth by

[1] Rawlinson's Herodotus, ii., p. 304.
[2] Milman, i., p. 118.

the hand of Moses and Aaron. But the time
had come for mercy and for judgment: the sins
of those who held the Land of Promise were
crying aloud for punishment; the events of
centuries had been paving the way for its occupation by the Chosen People; and "God heard
their groaning: and God remembered.His covenant with Abraham, with Isaac, and with Jacob,
and He saved them from the hand of him that
hated them, and redeemed them from the hand
of the enemy."

In this sketch of the sojourn of Israel in
Egypt, needful to show the influences that were
moulding the Canaanite tribes, I have followed
in the main Dean Milman (whose view does not
differ much from those of Bunsen, Brugsch, and
other excellent authorities), though not without
a careful consideration of the schemes of Lenormant, Poole, and Wilkinson. The first of these
supposes that Joseph was taken into favour by
one of the shepherd kings; but the reasons
already adduced seem sufficient to disprove this.
Sir Gardner Wilkinson (with Ewald) makes the
Exodus to happen towards the close of the
eighteenth dynasty. But it is inconceivable,

if this were the case, that even in the very
fragmentary state of the history given us by the
books of Joshua and Judges, we should find no
allusions in them to the numerous invasions of
Canaan by Seti and Rameses II. Mr. Poole's
theory, which places both the arrival of Joseph
and the Exodus within the period of the Hyksos
kings, seems to present more difficulties than any
other. The theory of Lepsius, which places the
arrival of Abraham after the accession of the
eighteenth dynasty, has not received the adhesion of any scholar of note in England, France,
or Germany.

Canon Cook, in an Essay on the Bearings of
Egyptian History upon the Pentateuch (in the
"Speaker's Commentary," vol. i., pp. 443—475),
published since this essay was written, contends
that not only the visit of Abraham, but also the
migration under Jacob, is to be placed before
the invasion of the Hyksos kings, and that the
Exodus took place under Thothmes II. (of
the eighteenth dynasty). There is very much
evidence in favour of this view, but it does not
seem to me on the whole preferable to that
which has here been adopted.

CHAPTER II.

HISTORICAL SKETCH OF THE RELATIONS BETWEEN PHŒNICIA AND ISRAEL.

Canaan at the time of its Conquest—Extent of the Conquest—
Relations with the Phœnician Cities under the Judges—
Under the Kings—History of Tyre up to the Captivity of
Judah.

IT has been said above, that we find a great
change had passed over the land of Canaan
between the departure of Jacob and the invasion
of Joshua. The revolution had no doubt been
slow, but its effects were very visible. Like the
Hebrews themselves, the Canaanites had been a
purely pastoral people, but now they were developing agriculture ; the vine and the olive were
already widely cultivated, and fenced cities' were
common.[1] A similar change was seen in their
political relations to each other. The kings with

[1] Milman, i., p. 219.

whom Jacob met were still the patriarchal heads of tribes. In the time of Joshua we find either local princes, taking their titles from the cities that were the centres of government, or else, as in the case of Gibeon, an aristocratic republic already established.[1] The art of war had greatly developed, and in the course of the continual wars in which these tribes were engaged, either against the Egyptian invader, or under his banners, against their powerful Khita brethren of the north, abundant experience had been gained. It is difficult to say whether the war-chariot was brought to them from Egypt, or whether it was not rather their original possession, and was communicated to the Egyptians by the shepherd kings. It is certain that the horse is never represented on any sculpture of a date prior to the Hyksos dynasty.[2] Be this as it may, their horses and chariots very many seem to have proved at this time their main reliance in war. But the independent spirit of the Semitic race, always averse to organization, and never forgetting that its true centre was the tent and the tribe,[3] kept the various Canaanite nations severed from each

[1] Ewald, i., p. 241.   [3] Rénan, p. 13.
[2] Rawlinson's Herodotus, ii.

other, each in a defiant isolation, yielding but
incompletely even to the terror of a foreign invasion.[1] We find the numerous cities of the
land,[2] excluding such as were still held by the
warlike and savage aborigines, loosely grouped
into four main divisions.[3] There are the Amorites,
or Highlanders, a fierce people (apparently the
farthest removed from the Canaanites proper)
" that dwelt in the mountains,[4] from the Scorpion
Range, south of the Dead Sea, to the hills of
Judah. The Hittites are their neighbours,
dwelling in the valleys, lovers of refinement at
an early period, and living in well-ordered communities possessing national assemblies."[5] The
fertile lowlands by the course of the Jordan, and
along the coast of the Mediterranean, are held by
the Canaanites,[6] who, as possessors of the choicest
of the land, and by far the best known to
foreigners, often gave their name to the whole of

[1] Lenormant, ii., p. 151.
[2] The thirty-one cities that are mentioned in Joshua
xii. 9, 24, do not include even all that we have mentioned
in the course of the book. (Ewald, ii., p. 231, *sq.*)
[3] Ewald, i., pp. 234—237.
[4] Joshua x. 6, cp. Deut. i. 44.
[5] Ewald, *u. s.*
[6] On χαναάν = *terra depressa*, from the verb כָּנַע, cp.
Movers, ii., p. 6.

the population of the country. These also were much more addicted to commerce than to war, in this resembling the fourth main division, the Hivvites (*Ewald*) of the midland region, whose principal city seems to have been the flourishing, wealthy, but timorous Gibeon. Every hint that we have points to a high state of civilization as already existing;[1] but this was accompanied with the grossest moral depravity. A fitter occasion will be afterwards found (in the section on the religious influence of Phœnicia) for discussing the causes that led to this condition. It is sufficient now to notice that the Biblical narrative always uses the strongest language in speaking of the frightful degradation of the Canaanites,[2] which made the Lord to abhor them;[3] and which was at once the necessary and the sufficient reason for the merciless destruction that the children of Israel were commanded to bring upon them.[4]

One other nation in the land of Canaan seems

[1] See especially Bochart's remarks on Kirjath-Sepher, "The City of Books," and Keil on Joshua x. 38.

[2] Lev. xviii. 3, xx. 23.

[3] Deut. ix. 5, xii. 31, etc., etc.

[4] The absolute need for such terrible severity has been often showed by Christian apologists, against the cavils

to have possessed already at least a portion of
the district that afterwards bore its name. The
uncertainty which, after all that has yet been
done by the scholars of Germany, still perplexes
our views of the early ethnology of the Land of
Promise, is nowhere so great as in the case of
the Philistines. But, on the whole, the fragmentary hints, which are all that we have upon
the subject, seem to point to the conclusion that,
even at the time of the Exodus, the southern
coast of Palestine bore already the name of
Philistia, and even then was not without those
fortress cities that afterwards formed the nucleus
of the strength of the Philistines.[1] But in these
early times they seem to have been but weak,
and under the yoke of the alien Canaanites, to
whom they were always bitterly hostile.[2] And
even after the days of Joshua, though strength-

of unbelievers ; but never more forcibly than by Arnold,
Sermons, vol. vi., pp. 35—37.

[1] Ewald, i., p. 245.

[2] We shall have occasion to notice afterwards the heavy
blows that they inflicted on the power of Sidon. By
using the term " alien," I do not mean to imply my assent
to the theory of Hitzig (*Urgeschichte und Mythologie der
Philistäer*, Leipzig, 1845), who finds in the Philistines an
offshoot of the Pelasgi. His arguments do not seem to
me at all convincing, and unless M. Stark,—whose *Fors-*

ened by numerous immigrants from their earlier
home in Crete, they broke their power by dashing
fruitlessly against the vastly superior forces of
Egypt, then ruled by Rameses III.[1] It was not
till the rapid decline of the Egyptian power had
left them free from even a nominal supremacy,
that, aided again by fresh accessions, they were
able to establish themselves securely, and reta-
liate in full measure for all the oppression that
they had endured. At the time of the invasion
of Joshua they probably formed but a small portion of the composite population of the southern
coast land, the greater part of which was constituted by the peaceful agricultural Avvim, and
the numerous but unaggressive and commercial
Canaanites.[2]

Such was the general distribution of the
various earlier inhabitants, when the children of
Israel crossed the borders of the Land of Promise. There is no occasion for us to review the
several stages of the invasion and conquest.

chungen, referred to by M. Lenormant (i., p. 123), I have
not been able to consult,—has others of greater force
to bring forward, it appears much safer to follow Ewald
and Movers in considering them a Semitic people. Lenormant follows Hitzig.

[1] Lenormant, i., p. 124.   [2] Ewald, i., p. 248.

But one point, which has been often overlooked, deserves a passing glance. The strategy of the leader of " the host of the Lord " (Jahveh) was, consciously or unconsciously, of the highest order. Had the attack been made upon the southern frontier, the invaders would have found before them an ever-increasing mass of enemies, and the successive mountain-ranges of Hebron, of Jerusalem, and of Ephraim. But when the Jordan was crossed near Jericho, that frontier fortress captured, and the passes secured by the ambuscade that destroyed the city of Ai, Joshua was able to drive his army like a wedge into the very heart of the hostile country, and strike his blows right and left at the isolated divisions of the enemy.[1]

The battles of Beth-horon and of Merom crushed the two great combinations of the Amorite and the Hittite kings, and the success of the invasion was secured. But six or seven years of fighting left the work but half accomplished. Many of the strongest posts in the country still remained in the hands of the Canaanites, and, curiously reversing the usual

[1] See Stanley, i., p. 237, and M. Chevallier in Lenormant, i., p. 111.

Canaänites, and, curiously reversing the usual issue of an irruption of invaders that show themselves the stronger in battle, the plains continued to be held by their earlier occupants. The enthusiasm of the Hebrew people for the land in which their fathers were buried, the longing of the desert-hardened warriors[1] for "the good land, the land of brooks of water, of fountains and depths, that spring out of valleys and hills ; the land of wheat and barley, and vines and fig-trees and pomegranates ; the land of oil olive, and honey ;" their firm belief that the LORD their God was leading them into the possession of this beautiful home,—all these influences tended to make their onset irresistible. The rude weapons and primitive tactics of the children of Israel swept before them the serried and confederate masses that followed the Canaanitish kings. But such an invasion could hardly be more at first than a razzia.[2] We have reason, indeed, to suppose that in the panic caused by the first great victories of Joshua, the

---

[1] On the results of the desert training there are words well worth noting in Mr. Baldwin Brown's " Soul's Exodus," pp. 322—326.

[2] Ewald, ii., p. 241.

3

Canaanites on all sides gave in their submission ; and it is probable that even Sidon, " the eldest-born of Canaan," did not refuse to pay homage to the conquering invaders.   At least we find that afterwards the rightful territory of Israel is assumed to extend over Sidon and its surrounding cities.[1]   But if there was ever a temporary submission, its effects were very transient ; and we find the inhabitants of Phœnicia proper "living quiet and secure,"[1] undisturbed by the neighbouring tribes of Israel.[2]   They had now been settled for a long time in the cities of the coast.   We are able to determine, with tolerable exactness, the date of their arrival there by the help of one of the most curious and valuable documents that have been given to the world in the progress of hieroglyphic interpretation. A hieratic papyrus, translated by M. Chabas, contains the report of an Egyptian officer, sent by Amenembe I., a king of the twelfth dynasty, to examine into the condition of the principalities of Edom and Tennu, then dependent on Egypt, and to bring back information upon the neighbouring tribes ; and it admits of proof that none of the nations mentioned in this most

1 Judges i. 31.   2 Judges xviii. 7.

interesting document belonged to the Canaanite race.[1]

On the other hand, on the arrival of Abraham in the Land of Promise, we find that "the Canaanite and the Perizzite *then* dwelt in the land,"[2] a form of expression from which we may probably deduce that they had not long been there. Whence they came, is another of the points much disputed by the best authorities. All the native traditions that are preserved to us of course represent them as autochthonous ; but when we find this the case with people like the Greeks, who can be shown most clearly to be immigrants,[3] such statements cannot weigh very much in the balance of the historian. The Greek authorities are unanimous in pointing to the banks of the Erythræan Sea, or Persian Gulf, as the original home of the nation.[4] The close analogy in many respects between the religion and civilization of Phœnicia and of

[1] Lenormant, ii., p. 148. [2] Gen. xiii. 7.

[3] On this point the theories of Dr. E. Curtius (see especially i., pp. 62—64, of Prof. Ward's translation) deserve very careful consideration.

[4] Movers, ii., 1, pp. 38—48. The Bishop of Ely (on Gen. x. 6) confuses the Erythræum Mare with the modern Red Sea.

Babylon, each partaking of a very marked
Cushite character, is evidence in the same
direction. M. Rénan's conclusion is that the
Phœnician people were the first to issue from
the common cradle of the Semitic race,—that is,
the mountains of Kurdistan,—and that it was
in the fertile plains of the lower Euphrates
that they developed a civilization which in
its departure from the simpler manners and
purer life of their pastoral brethren, made
them afterwards the objects of their exe-
cration.[1] M. Lenormant contents himself with
tracing them to the basin of the Euphrates,
and ascribes their expulsion thence to the Aryan
invasion of Babylonia, just at the time to which
other evidence points as the date of their invasion
of Palestine.[2] Movers, on the contrary, accepts
the tradition that their earliest settlements were
on the coast of the Mediterranean ; but his
arguments do not appear convincing, and he
is throughout disposed to assign far too much
weight to uncertain deductions from an obscure
mythology ; and, on the whole, we may agree
with Mr. Kenrick that in favour of the statements
of Herodotus, Justin, and Strabo, "we have a

[1] Rénan, p. 186.   [2] ii., pp. 23—48.

body of evidence which it would not be safe to set aside."[1]   The stock to which they belonged is another perplexing question, which cannot probably be set at rest until we have arrived at something more like agreement as to the terms to be employed in ethnology.   The Biblical account in Genesis x. places them among the descendants of Ham, while the language that they spoke is evidently Semitic.   The difficulty vanishes if we may suppose, with Mr. Kenrick, that the classification in Genesis is based upon colour, which would prevent the *red* Phœnicians from being ranked with the paler Semites.   And .we can easily understand then how Canaan should be held to be the brother of Mizraim, if we remember how constantly the Egyptian monuments preserve the marked difference of

---

[1] Phœnicia, p. 52 ; cp. the preceding pages.   Professor Rawlinson (Herodotus, Book vii., App. ii.) accepts the tradition of an immigration of the Phœnicians, but places it as late as the thirteenth century B.C.   This must stand or fall with his rejection of the identity of the Phœnicians and the Canaanites ; the only authorities for the view that has here been maintained which he discusses are Bochart and Kenrick ; but he has also to deal with Gesenius, Movers, Bunsen, Ewald, Rénan, and Lenormant, a consensus of authority which is not easily shaken, and which Dr. Dyer (in Dict. Geog.) and Mr. Twisleton are content to follow. .

tint between the native warriors and their Semitic
enemies. Knobel and Hitzig (quoted by Rénan,
p. 52,) attempt to confirm this view by the etymology of the names Shem, Ham, and Japhet,
but apparently with little success. It is perhaps
better, with M. Rénan, to regard the table of
nations in Genesis as simply geographical. One
of the principal difficulties in ancient ethnology
arises from the very lax notions which all our
authorities seem to have had upon the principles
of classification, and the arbitrary manner in
which they conjoin or dissever tribes upon no
intelligible grounds. Certainly they were not
guided by any comparative study of languages,.
for it has been reserved for later scholars to dis-
cern, under superficial divergences, the essential
identity of kindred tongues. But if we regard
Japhet, Shem, and Ham as representing the
northern, central, and southern zones of population respectively,[1] we shall not find any difficulty
in understanding how a Semitic nation like the
Phœnicians, that had dwelt in the midst of
Hamite tribes, and probably acquired no small
share of their habits and morals, should have
been classed among them. The same is probably

[1] Rénan, p. 50.

the case with the Cushites, who seem to have been nearly connected with the Phœnicians ; for although they too are placed among the descend-ants of Ham, it is certain that in the countries that bore this name Semitic dialects were spoken from a very high antiquity.[1] At any rate, it is much more easy to conceive of a change of manners and beliefs, than it is to imagine a nation changing its language.[2]

But be all this as it may, it is certain that the children of Israel on their arrival in the Land of Promise found the coast of Phœnicia studded with thriving commercial cities. " The strong city Tyre " is mentioned first in Joshua xix. 29, but Sidon is known to Jacob at the time of the blessing of his children. And even Sidon, ac-cording to the native tradition, was compelled to yield in antiquity to Byblus and Berytus, the towns of a race distinct from the Sidonian Canaanites, and at this time independent of them.[3] Berytus, the modern Beirût, may indeed

[1] Renan, p. 52, note i.; cp. p. 186.
[2] The Bishop of Ely (in the Speaker's Commentary, Gen. x. 6) reverses this statement, and supposes that the Canaanites were of Hamite origin, but adopted a Semitic language from some (purely imaginary) Semitic race, whom they found in possession of Palestine.
[3] Movers, ii., pp. 105—113.

contest with Damascus the honour of being the
oldest city in the world that still continues to
prosper. But as far as the Jewish tradition
carries us back, Sidon takes its place at the
head of the Phœnician cities ; and this is the
true interpretation of the figure of speech that
makes Sidon " the eldest-born of Canaan."[1]
Tyre, though as we have seen it was founded
before the invasion of the Israelites, was still in
a state of dependence on the mother-state ; and
the name of Sidon, as we see from the limits
assigned to the tribe of Zebulon, was applied
to the whole sea-coast, as far to the south as
Carmel.

We may therefore figure to ourselves the
strip of coast-land covered by the name " Phœnicia "[2] tenanted at this time by a people un-
questionably allied very closely to the Canaanites
of the interior, but distinguished from them
by striking differences of manners, and a still
more advanced and peaceful civilization. Confined to a narrow strip of land by the spurs of

---

[1] Movers, ii., pp. 89—92.

[2] Movers (ii., p. 15) has collected abundance of evidence
to show that both " Canaan " and " Phœnicia " (or more
properly Phœnice [Winer, RWB., s. v.]) were used in
a wider and a narrower sense.

Lebanon, which served at the same time to protect them to a great extent from incursions from the east, the Sidonian people devoted themselves at first to the fisheries from which they drew their name.[1] But the numerous harbours with which the coast was furnished, tempted them to venture by degrees on longer voyages than had ever been tried before. Egypt, then under the rule of the kindred Hyksos kings, was naturally the first country with which they established commercial relations, and at a very early age these had grown into great importance. Bunsen may possibly have over-estimated the effects of the intimate connection which resulted ; but we cannot doubt that the intercourse of the Phœnicians with the country that was then in the forefront of the civilization of the world, must have had a very powerful influence in developing the arts and sciences amongst them. Whether it was from this quarter that the Phœnician alphabet was derived, is a point on which it is much less easy to arrive at a satisfactory conclusion : *adhuc sub iudice lis est.* Ewald maintains, *more suo* undoubtingly, that this inestimable benefit is due

[1] Cp. Movers, ii., p. 86, note (8).

to the shepherd kings of Avaris, who obtained
it by a modification of the Egyptian hieratic
writing,[1] and the same view fundamentally is
supported by a number of *savants*, referred to
by M. Rénan.[2] But that distinguished scholar
is himself of the opinion that the alphabet of
twenty-two letters had its origin in Babylon,
where the earliest specimens of it, he thinks, are
found ;[3] and that the Phœnicians, here as in so
many other points, were simply the medium
through which the discoveries of Babylon passed
into the western world.[4] This view does not
appear to harmonize with the admitted fact, that
the children of Israel were ignorant of the art
of writing when they went down into Egypt,
and had acquired the knowledge of it by the
time of the Exodus.[5] So that we are led to agree
with M. Rénan that "l'origine de l'écriture, chez

---

[1] Ewald, ii., p. 7 (E. T.), cp. i., p. 49.

[2] p. 113.

[3] p. 72.

[4] p. 115. It is very noteworthy that the names of the
letters point to an origin among a pastoral rather than a
commercial people. See Dict. Bible, iii. 1790*b*.

[5] This is abundantly proved by Rénan, p. 117, and
Ewald, i., p. 47. There is not a single reference to writing
of any kind in the book of Genesis. It is first distinctly
mentioned in Ex. xvii. 14.

les Semites comme chez tous les peuples, se cache dans une profonde nuit." At any rate we may be certain, that when the Israelites entered the Holy Land, the Phœnicians were already carrying this priceless treasure where-ever their commerce spread, though it was not till centuries after that the Greeks had made themselves familiar with its value.[1] The nature and effects of this commerce will have to be considered more at length in a subsequent section of this essay. .

From the accession of the eighteenth dynasty, the Sidonians appear to have been tributaries of the Egyptians, and to have remained content with a nominal dependence, which left them free to pursue their peaceful avocations in un-disturbed security. We do not find the names of any one of their cities recorded in the lists of conquered rebels, which adorn the walls of the temples of Thothmes III., Seti I., and Rameses II. While all the other Canaanitish tribes were fur-nishing constant material for the triumphs of

[1] This seems one (we are tempted to write *the* one) definite conclusion which has resulted from the vast mass of controversial writing, originating in the publication of F. A. Wolf's famous Prolegomena.

the Egyptian arms, the Sidonians seem to have severed themselves entirely from their brethren of the inland districts, and the frequent mention made of them speaks only of the splendour of their arts and the magnitude of their tribute. In another most interesting account of the country, which, like the one already quoted, has been made accessible to us by M. Chabas, we have valuable notices of the various Phœnician cities. The account is thrown into the form of an imaginary journey made through the land by an Egyptian officer towards the end of the reign of Rameses II., and throughout the traveller speaks as if he were on Egyptian soil, " travelling with as much freedom and security as if he had been in the Nile valley, and even, by virtue of his functions, exercising some authority."[1]

It is evident that the kings of Egypt, like the kings of Persia a thousand years later, felt that they needed the services of the Phœnician marine, and therefore treated these valued vassals with marked lenity and favour, while they in their turn, content with an almost nominal subjection that left them the full enjoyment of their national worship, laws, and

[1] Lenormant, ii., pp. 160, 161.

customs, showed no desire to throw off the yoke that lay so lightly. One result of this sagacious mercantile policy was the rise of the wealth and influence of Sidon to its culminating point. This was the period when, as Humboldt says, "their flag waved at once in Britain and the Indian Ocean." Free as yet from the competition of the bold Ionian mariners, who were soon to drive them and their colonists alike from the western waters of the Mediterranean, they had no rivals in a trade, whose profits were sometimes almost fabulous.[1] Aristotle tells us of one visit to Tartessus, in which for the oil and other products of little value with which they had laden their vessels, they received so much silver that they were unable to carry it, and at last cut off the masses of lead which had served them as anchors, and substituted silver in the place of them. The science of comparative mythology forbids us to follow M. Lenormant in regarding the story of the Golden Fleece as *intended* to symbolize the wealth that they drew from their commerce with the Euxine, but the type is not the less happy because very far

[1] De Mir. Ausc., p. 147 (quoted by Mr. Kenrick, p. 211).

from the original meaning of the myth.[1] When, centuries later, the gold of Colchis, the tin of the Caucasus, and the steel of the barbarous Chalybes found their way to the markets of Greece in the ships of Chalcis or Athens, instead of the Sidonian galleys, no image could be more than adequate to express the gain to the people of Hellas.

Another, and, for our present purpose, a yet more important result of this contented acquiescence in the suzerainty of Egypt on the part of the Phœnicians, was the extent to which it divided their interests from those of the other Canaanitish nations. Even in the great confederacy headed by Jabin, king of Hazor, we find them taking no part; and when this was broken at the battle of Merom, the fugitives are pursued to the borders of "great Sidon" (Josh. xi. 8), but there the pursuit apparently ends. Accustomed as they were to see the armies of Egypt pour into the country of Canaan, year after year, they might well look with comparative indifference on the progress of a new invader. This peaceful relation be-

[1] Cp. Cox's Mythology of the Aryan Nations, ii., pp. 150—153.

tween the Israelites and the Phœnicians would
be promoted by the position and interests of
both the nations.[1] The district of Sidon had
apparently been included in the earliest scheme
of conquest. But it had not fallen to the lot of
either of the two most powerful and warlike
tribes, Judah and Ephraim ; it was destined for
the feebler and less energetic, Asher, Zebulon,
Issachar, and Naphtali. The impetuous rush of
the hardy warriors of the desert, thirsting for
the blessings of the Promised Land, had spent
itself in its early efforts, and the northern tribes
were well contented with the marvellous fertility
of the plain of Esdraelon,[2] which probably furnished abundant supplies for their scantier numbers. The Phœnicians, on the other hand,
would have the strongest inducements to live
on terms of amity with their new neighbours. We
shall have occasion to notice hereafter how large
a portion of their commerce consisted in a carrying trade by land.[3] Now at the time when the
wave of invasion was rolling towards the borders

---

[1] Movers, ii., pp. 305, 599.

[2] See Stanley's Sinai and Palestine, p. 348, *sq.*

[3] This is fully discussed by Movers, vol. ii., part 3, pp.
128—147, and 200—313.

of Phœnicia, it had already swept over southern and central Palestine, and if the Canaanites had not yet been extirpated from the land, at least their kingdoms had been broken up, and their power completely crippled. The great lines of traffic with Egypt, Arabia, Babylon, and Assyria were in the hands of the invaders, and any hostilities with them must necessarily have caused a ruinous suspension of commerce.[1] Perhaps we may find a further reason for the policy that was adopted, in the fact that just before the arrival of the Israelites there seems to have been a great extension of the power of the Amorites,[2] so that, in southern Canaan at any rate, it was with these especially that the invaders came into contact. But we have seen already that of all the population of Palestine (excluding the remnants of the barbarous aborigines), the Amorites were those who were furthest removed from the Phœnicians, and those, in consequence, with whom they would have least sympathy. The " fat bread " and " royal dainties " of Asher[3] would have far more attractions for the teeming

---

[1] Movers, ii., p. 305.
[2] Movers, ii., pp. 68, 599.
[3] Gen. xlix. 20.

population of the Sidonian coast than any half-
recognized claims of kindred ; and the people
whose descendants long after "were nourished
by the king's country,"[1] would be careful not to
close their markets against the grain of Galilee.

Still we must not go so far as Mr. Kenrick,
and say that the settlement of the Israelites in
Canaan "produced no visible effect on the
condition of the Phœnician cities."[2] We may
be sure that no small number of those who
" fled from before the face of the robber Joshua,
the son of Nun,"[3] would take refuge in the
kindred towns on the coast, and so, by increasing
the pressure of a population already super-
abundant, give rise to colonies, in the strict
sense of the term, as distinguished from the
trading posts and commercial factories which
were all that had previously been established.
The dense obscurity which envelops the early
history of Greece, and the hopelessness of all
attempts to establish a trustworthy system of

[1] Acts xii. 20.
[2] Phœnicia, p. 63.
[3] The genuineness of the celebrated inscription in
Mauretania, reported by Procopius to contain these words,
has been disproved by recent scholars. See Kenrick,
pp. 67, 68 ; Ewald, ii., p. 230.

4

chronology before the date of the first Olympiad,
prevent us from speaking here with any confidence ; but it is at least possible that one of
these was that which Cadmus is said to have
led to Thebes ;[1] and the best authorities (Movers
and Munk) are willing to assign to this period
some of the earliest settlements in Africa,[2] those
to which the numerous cities of the Liby-
Phœnicians owe their origin.   And further, we
may gladly accept the theory of Ewald, that
"the nobler part of the [Canaanite] nation,
unable longer to maintain themselves in the
interior, gathered their forces together on the
northern sea-coast for a new and more vigorous
life, and thus the regenerated remnant of the
people gained for themselves an honourable
place in the history of the world."[3]

There is evidence, however, to show that the
superiority of the Israelite arms was soon

---

[1] Even Mr. Cox (Mythology of the Aryans, ii., 86, note)
is willing to admit that the manifest connection of Kadmos
with Semitic Kedem, " the East," is strong evidence for
such a colonization, and it was enough to satisfy the
scepticism of Niebuhr.   But the date is a very different
thing from the fact.   Cp. Grote, ii., p. 48.

[2] Lenormant, ii., pp. 169—172.

[3] Ewald, i., p. 242.

changed into something very like subjection. Not only did the tribe of Asher fail to "drive out the inhabitants of Accho, of Sidon,"[1] and of the other Phœnician cities, but we find that they "dwelt among the Canaanites, the inhabitants of the land," a phrase in which Movers[2] (from comparing other instances in which it is used) finds indications of at least a nominal submission.[3] "The dainties of the king" ascribed to the same tribe in the blessing of Jacob, he regards as a tribute paid to the court of Sidon, and finds traces in the after-history of the tribe of the contempt which this subservience awakened.[4] In the language used of Issachar in the same grand poem, we seem to have a reference to the position of a tribe bordering on a commercial nation, and acting as the transporters of their wares. Zebulon and Naphtali, in the same way, are brought into a close connection, probably one of partial dependence, with Phœnicia; and on the whole the northern Israelites during this obscure period appear as a kind of Metœci, with the possession of the land secured to them, but also with certain burdens

---

[1] Judges i. 31.
[2] ii., 1, p. 307, *sq.*
[3] Gen. xlix. 19.
[4] 1 Kings ix. 13.

laid upon them. From what we know of the
policy of the Phœnician colonies in similar
cases, we can readily conceive that these burdens were sometimes made to press very
heavily ; and it causes us no surprise when
we find the Sidonians mentioned among the
oppressors of Israel, in the touching record of
the faithlessness of the chosen people, and the
tender compassion of the Lord, when " His soul
was grieved for the misery of Israel." [1] The
charge of Amos (i. 9) that Tyre "had not
remembered the covenant of brethren, but
delivered up the whole captivity to Edom," [2] may
even point to a condition of vassalage, modified
by the stipulation that none of the children of
Israel should be carried away out of their own
boundaries.

Movers has gleaned one hint upon the condition of these vassals from a very unexpected
quarter. Aristophanes (Aves, 505—507) has
these lines :—

Πεισθ. χὤπόθ' ὁ κόκκυς εἴποι κόκκυ, τότ' ἂν οἱ Φοίνικες ἅπαντες
      τοὺς πυροὺς ἂν καὶ τὰς κριθὰς ἐν τοῖς πεδίοις ἐθέριζον.
Εὐελπ. τοῦτ' ἄρ' ἐκεῖν' ἦν τοῦπος ἀληθῶς. κόκκυ, ψωλοί, πεδίονδε.

The scholiasts here inform us that in Phœ-

---

[1] Judges x. 12, 16.   [2] Cp. Joel iii. 6, 8.

nicia the cuckoo appears at the time of harvest, while in Greece the harvest is of course later,[1] so that the proverb is of Phœnician origin. But ψωλοὶ is here evidently a term of reproach, and in this sense would not have been applied by the Phœnicians to themselves. Besides which, the practice of circumcision seems to have been confined to a part of Phœnicia, and not to have been universal even there.[2] Hence the phrase was probably applied to serfs, compelled to labour in the fields, to whom the epithet would be appropriate ; and we know of none such but the Hebrews. This interpretation is strongly confirmed by the explanation given in Suidas (*s. v.* θύραζε) of the similar proverbial phrase θύραζε Κᾶρες, οὐκέτ᾽ ᾽Ανθεστήρια.[3] Whatever may be the value of this argument—and it is certainly greatly diminished by the fact that we have not the faintest indication of the period at which it originated—there seems to be evidence enough to show that, while Phœnicia

[1] Cp. Hesiod, Op. 457.

[2] On this point Movers refers to his article on the Phœnicians in Ersch and Gruber, p. 421. Herod., ii., 104, is not sufficient to disprove this view.

[3] Movers has overlooked this, but it is quoted in Kock's note, *ad loc.*

remained at peace with the nation of Israel, some portions at least of the weaker northern tribes were brought, originally perhaps by their own action, into a state of dependence approaching to vassalage.[1]

The curtain now falls upon Phœnicia, at least so far as the Jewish annals are concerned, and we get no further glimpses of the cities of the coast, except in one passing reference to their "quiet and secure life," until the establishment of the monarchy. This is undoubtedly due in a measure to the very fragmentary condition of the records of the time preserved to us. The composer of the Book of Judges was much more careful to recount the striking instances of the punishment that had fallen upon the people for their sins, and the wonderful deliverances granted to them, when they turned again in penitence to Jahveh, than he was to draw up a complete chronological history. And if the opinion of Ewald be correct, that the " Book of Covenants," on which the Book of Judges as we have it now was based, was written by an author belonging to the tribe of Judah,[2] we can the

[1] Mainly from Movers, ii., 1, 302—315.
[2] Cp. i., p. 72 *ff*, and 140 *ff*.

more readily understand the paucity of our information upon all but the most striking events connected with Northern Palestine.

But all indications point to a peaceful alliance between the Phœnician cities and the tribes that bordered upon them.[1] Heeren (Historical Researches, ii., p. 117) has well brought out the importance of the corn supplies of Galilee to the wealthy mercantile towns of the coast, and we may believe that the absence of any mention of conflicts between the two nations is not solely due to the incompleteness of our chronicles of the period.

We are not left, however, without information from other sources to throw light on this period of darkness, and profane historians help us to understand the change that has taken place in the internal condition of Phœnicia when we find it next coming into prominence in the Hebrew annals. We learn from hieroglyphic inscriptions the immense importance attached by the Egyptian kings to a secure possession of the littoral region of Canaan, as forming the military road by which their armies advanced to the ever-recurring wars with the Khitas and

[1] Cp. Stanley, Sinai and Palestine, p. 363.

the other nations of Northern Syria.[1]   It may
indeed well be that the fear of a direct collision
with the power of Egypt was one of the principal causes that led the children of Israel to
abstain from any direct attack upon the cities of
the coast.   For as long as the road to the un-
subdued people of the North was still left open,
the Pharaohs were probably contented with a
merely nominal supremacy over the hilly inland
country, a supremacy which is not indeed
mentioned in the Biblical narrative, but to
which the circumstances of the case very decidedly point.[2]   It is at all events certain that
no mention is made of the conquests of Rameses
III. in the books of Joshua and of Judges,
though M. Biot has assigned them, on indubitable
astronomical evidence,[3] to the close of the four-
teenth century B.C., a period certainly included
in the time with which those books are concerned ; and, on the other hand, the very full
monumental record of these conquests in the
temple of Medinet Abou, contains no reference
to the children of Israel.   But the tablets of

[1] Lenormant, i., p. 264, *et sæpius.*
[2] *Ib.,* p. 263.
[3] *Ib.,* p. 268, note.

this temple depict many scenes from a war
which was indirectly of great importance to the
history both of Israel and of Phœnicia. Next to
the never-ending struggle with the Khitas, the
most important conflict that occupied the arms
of Rameses was that with the Philistines. We
have already had occasion to adduce reasons
for accepting the view of Ewald, that a portion
of this nation, though as yet in insignificant
numbers, had settled in the district, where their
presence afterwards was such a thorn in the side
of Israel. But now, apparently in alliance with
the Khitas, a much more numerous body had
arrived by sea, probably from the island of
Crete, and thrown themselves in the rear of the
army of Rameses. It was a national immigration rather than an invasion,—the sculptors
represent them as followed by numerous rude
waggons, drawn by oxen, containing their wives
and children,—and the veterans of the Pharaoh
gained an easy victory. Others who followed
them shared their fate. But Rameses, em-
barrassed with a nation on his hands, contented
himself with assigning to them the land
round Gaza, Ashdod, and Ascalon, in immediate proximity to strong Egyptian garrisons.

But after the reign of Rameses III. the power
of Egypt rapidly declined ; her Asiatic do-
minions threw off even her nominal supremacy,
and the Philistines soon developed into a warlike
and powerful people.[1] Augmented probably by
constant accessions from their earlier home,[2] in
the course of about a hundred years they succeeded in bringing the whole of Southern
Palestine under their power, and for half a
century ruled the Israelites of that region with
a rod of iron.[3] But they did not confine their
activity to the continent. They had never
forgotten the maritime skill that had brought
them into Canaan, and they seem to have
devoted themselves largely to piracy. This it
was, apparently, which brought them into conflict with the Phœnicians ; and a valuable
notice in Justin[4] tells us of the Sidonians that
" post multos deinde annos a rege Ascaloniorum

---

[1] In the monuments this nation is called *Khairetana*,
which Mr. Poole indentifies with the people of Crete, and
consequently, according to the best authorities, with the
Philistines. Cp. Rawlinson's Herodotus, ii., p. 298, with
Lenormant, i., p. 266, Dict. Bible, art. *Philistines* and
Cherethites, and Stanley, Sinai and Palestine, p. 256.

[2] Hitzig, Philistäer, § 100.

[3] Cp. Ewald, ii., 338.

[4] xviii. 3, 5 ; in Movers, ii. 1, p. 150.

expugnati, navibus appulsi Tyron urbem ante annum Troianæ cladis condiderunt." Justin's date for the capture of Troy is probably B.C. 1208,[1] so that we are able to fix with precision the time of the transfer of the hegemony of Phœnicia from Sidon to Tyre. At the same time we must notice that the words of Justin need some qualification. Tyre, as we have seen already, was known in the time of Joshua, and the priests of the temple of Melkarth there informed Herodotus,[2] that the city had been founded 2,300 years before his time, a claim which Movers is disposed to allow :[3] Sidon, again, if ever destroyed, was soon rebuilt, and though it never regained its position as first of the Phœnician cities, still it had a long career of great prosperity. But henceforth it is Tyre, which is the capital of the cities of the coast, and Tyre whose kings are brought into immediate relation with Israel.

Again the curtain falls. The sacred narrative makes no mention of Phœnicia till the days of

[1] Cp. Kenrick, p. 342, Movers, ii., 1, p. 150—166. I cannot discover the authority on which Prof. Rawlinson (Manual, p. 39) adopts as the date B.C. 1050.

[2] ii., p. 44.

[3] ii., 1, pp. 134—137.

David ;[1] and all that we can gather from other
sources is a string of names that are mythical.
Phœnix, father of Cadmus and Europa, is a
personification of the country, or, according to
comparative mythologists, a still more shadowy
form, the lord of the purple region of the dawn.[2]
Belus is of course the god Baal ; and Agenor,
like Phaidimos, the Sidonian of Homer,[3] is the
Greek translation of the epithet of some deity,
probably Melkarth.[4]   But we are able to watch
the operation of the causes which were soon to
bring the kingdoms of Tyre and of Israel into
close connection with each other.   First among
them we must place the growth of the power
of the Philistines.   It does not appear that
after the campaign which resulted in the de-

[1] 1 Kings v. 1, vii. 14.
[2] Cox, Aryan Mythology, i., p. 438.
[3] Od. iv. 617.   The curious fact that Homer, though several times referring to Phœnicia and to the Sidonians, never
once mentions Tyre, may perhaps be best explained by
the hypothesis that he knew by tradition of a period when
Sidon was the leading city, and Tyre insignificant, and
that he uses the name of the former from a wish to give
an archaic colouring to his poem.   But there are not
many scholars who will see in this fact, with Mr. Gladstone (Juventus Mundi, p. 144), satisfactory evidence
that Homer wrote before the fall of Sidon.
[4] Kenrick, p. 347.

struction of Sidon they made any serious
attack upon Phœnicia. . The narrow and barren
strip of coast that lay between the Philis-
tian and Phœnician cities, the district round
Dor and Joppa, could have offered to a pastoral
and agricultural people like the Philistines no
attractions comparable to those of the fertile
land of Judah ;[1] and it was to this accordingly
that their arms were constantly directed. Still
we must consider their relations with the neighbours on the north to have been those of suspicion, if not of positive hostility. We have
indeed several passages from the later prophets
in which they are apparently spoken of as allies.[2]

[1] "The most striking and characteristic feature of
Philistia is its immense plain of cornfields, stretching
from the edge of the sandy tract right up to the very wall
of the hills of Judah, which look down its whole length
from north to south. These rich fields must have been
the great source at once of the power and of the value
of Philistia ; the cause of its frequent aggressions on
Israel, and of the ceaseless efforts of Israel to master
the territory."—Stanley, Sinai and Palestine, p. 258.

[2] Jer. xlvii. 4: "The day cometh to spoil all the Philistines, and to cut off from Tyrus and Zidon every helper
that remaineth." Joel iii. 4: "What have ye to do with
me, O Tyre, and Zidon, and all the coasts of Palestine."
Zech. ix. 3—5: "Tyrus did build herself a strong hold,
and heaped up silver and gold. . . . Behold, the Lord
will cast her out, and He will smite her power in the

But Movers[1] can hardly be right in assuming
from these that the friendly connection dates
from the period which we are now considering.
It is much more likely that it dates from the
time when the power of the Philistines had not
yet recovered from the heavy blows inflicted
upon it by David ; and the friendship with
Judah, if not with the northern kingdom, had
been broken off by the expulsion of the dynasty
of Hiram ; but at this earlier period an attitude
of jealousy is much more intelligible than one of
close alliance.[2]

Another fact of the time which contributed
to bring together Phœnicia and Israel, was the
decline of the two great empires that had
hitherto overshadowed them both from opposite
sides. We have already referred to the decline
of the Egyptian power under the twentieth
and twenty-first dynasties ; but a similar loss
of strength seems to have befallen the empire

sea; and she shall be devoured with fire. Ashkelon
shall see it, and fear ; Gaza also, and be very sorrowful,
and Ekron," etc.

[1] ii., 1, p. 316.

[2] We find them positively at war with each other at the
commencement of the reign of David. See Lenormant,
i., p. 137.

of Assyria, so that all her possessions west of
the Euphrates were taken from her by the conquering Khitas.[1] We can readily believe that
the way was thus made clear for the establishment of a strong, compact, and independent
monarchy in Palestine, and nothing would more
contribute to this than a good understanding
with the powerful league of maritime cities.
They in their turn would be ready enough to
accept a position of secure amity. " It must
have been with no common interest that the
surrounding nations looked out to see on what
prey the Lion of Judah, now about to issue from
his native lair, would make his first spring."[2]
And when, after crushing, for the time at
least, the power of the Philistines, the strength
of the new military organization of Israel was
turned upon the nations of the east and south;
when Edom, as a submissive slave, held the
sandal, which had been drawn off that the
monarch might wash his feet in Moab, as in a
basin destined for the vilest uses ;[3] when the king

---

[1] Lenormant, i., p. 376. On these Khitas or Khatti,
cp. Rawlinson's Herodotus, i., p. 379.

[2] Stanley, Jewish Church, ii., p. 79.

[3] Psalm cviii. 9 ; cp. Herod., ii., p. 172.

of Hamath, on the distant Orontes, became an
ally of the victorious David, we do not wonder
at finding Tyre contributing stores of cedar-
wood[1] to build him a house in the new capital of
the new and mighty empire.[2]

The friendly relations, then if not previously
established, lasted without interruption to the
close of the reign of Solomon. The honours
which the young King Hiram (only twenty-eight
years of age at the death of David)[3] had gladly
paid to the aged poet-king would be granted
not less willingly to his youthful successor, for
whom he seems to have entertained a strong
personal affection. And the similarity between
the positions of the two princes would have
tended further to cement this alliance. Hiram,
like David, had just established his throne
securely upon the ruins of the rule of the

[1] 2 Sam. v. 11.

[2] Eupolemus asserts that David conquered Hiram, and
made Phœnicia tributary, but in the silence of the Biblical narrative, which gives us such full details of the other
wars of David, this assertion cannot be accepted. Cp.
Movers, ii., 1, p. 332.

[3] Movers, ii., 1, p. 328. I do not know on what authority
Dean Stanley speaks of the "relation between the *old*
Phœnician and the young Israelite." Solomon cannot
well have been ten years younger than Hiram.

Shophetim, or judges, and raised his country to a position of power and independence which it had not previously enjoyed. And if his capital was not, like Jerusalem, a new acquisition, the extent to which he enlarged, strengthened, and beautified it made it practically a new creation.[1] The influence of this close connection will have to be considered afterwards; in this rapid historical survey it only claims a mention.

Within twenty years of the death of Hiram his dynasty had fallen. His grandson,[2] Abdastertus, had been murdered by the sons of his nurse, and the eldest of these had placed himself upon the throne. Movers identifies this revolution with one which Justin, with his usual disregard of chronology, puts much later, just before the capture of the city by Alexander. According to his view, this was an uprising of the mercenaries, aided by the numerous slaves and the poverty-stricken commons, against the rule of the patrician houses, resembling in its causes, and probably also in the horrors with which it

---

[1] Cp. Kenrick's Phœnicia, pp. 348—354; Movers, ii., 1, p. 329.

[2] Lenormant writes the name Abdastoreth; I do not know on what authority.

was accompanied, the terrible insurrections of
the mercenaries and the Liby-Phœnicians against
the tyranny of the Carthaginian plutocracy. The
reign of disorder appears to have lasted twelve
years, and to have had for its natural results the
expulsion of many noble families, who probably
fled to the colonies already existing, or founded
new ones, and constant wars with the neighbouring cities that still retained their aristocratic
constitutions.[1] It is an ingenious and probable
conjecture of M. Lenormant that Shishak, king
of Egypt, who had contributed to the great rebellion in Israel by the encouragement which he
gave to Jeroboam, and who was at the time
meditating an invasion of Palestine, may have
been the author of the downfall of the dynasty
of Hiram. After the restitution of the royal
house in the person of Astartus, another grandson of Hiram, the numerous irregularities in
the succession show how severely the period of
anarchy had strained the Tyrian constitution ;
and during the time of disorder in the northern
kingdom marked by the murders of Nadab,
Elah, Zimri, and Tibni, hardly less disorder

[1] Movers, ii., 1, p. 342.

seems to have reigned in Tyre.[1] In thirty-three
years we find five rulers, not one of whom was
succeeded by his natural heir. The establishment of a lasting dynasty by Omri was nearly
contemporaneous with the accession of Ithobaal
to the throne of Tyre. It is probable that the
latter was the rightful representative of the race
of Hiram ; at least, we know that he held the
priesthood of Astarte, which was confined to the
royal family, and the security of his possession
of the throne seems some evidence of the legality
of his claim to it.[2] The marriage of his daughter
Jezebel (more correctly Isebel) to the son of
Omri, Ahab, was only a mark of the close connection which would naturally be renewed as
soon as the two neighbouring nations found
themselves again under settled government.
To the important commercial relations, of
which we have already spoken, was now added

[1] For the period between the accession of Hiram and
the flight of Elissa (980—826 according to Movers), we
have unusually trustworthy authorities in the numerous
fragments of the native historians, Dius and Menander,
quoted by Josephus, Antiq. viii. 5, 3, and in Apion. i., 17,
18. Cp. Movers, ii., 1, pp. 190, 191, where they are ex-
tracted.

[2] Movers, ii., 1, p. 345, but cp. against this Ewald, iii.,
p. 170.

the need of a defensive alliance against the
growing and aggressive power of the kingdom
of Syria, whose capital was Damascus. And
we shall not be wrong, I think, in seeing with
Movers,[1] in this marriage an instance of the
policy, pursued with so much success by the
Phœnicians of Carthage, who again and again
bound the native princes to them by links of
affinity and by the powerful influence of their
brilliant and beautiful women. Certainly the
force of character, cunning, boldness, and regal
pride even in the ' hour of death, shown . by
Jezebel, cannot but remind us of many stories
told us of Dido, of Sophonisba, of the wife of
Hasdrubal in the final siege of Carthage.

It is curious that we find no trace of any
attempt on the part of the king of Tyre,
Mattan,[2] the grandson of Ethbaal, to attempt
to revenge upon Jehu the murder of his aunt
Jezebel, and the massacre of the worshippers of
Baal in the temple of Samaria. This may be
partly due to the peaceful policy of Phœnicia.

---

[1] ii., 1, p. 347.

[2] On the various forms of this name, identical with the
Muttines of Livy (xxv. 40, 41, ed. Weissenborn), see
Movers, ii., 1, p. 353, note 64, and Mommsen, ii., p. 149.

But it is at least a singular coincidence, if
nothing more, that we find in the very year in
which Jehu ascended the throne, an expedition
of Shalmaneser, which resulted in the payment
of tribute by Tyre, Sidon, and Jebal, and also
the record[1] of a valuable present made by
Jehu to the Assyrian monarch. It is probable
that Shalmaneser would not readily allow an
attack to be made on a valued tributary. But,
again, it is all but certain that the internal dis-
sensions must have already begun which finally
led to the expulsion of Elessar,[2] and so to the
foundation of Carthage. Movers has collected
much evidence to show that this movement, of
such interest not only to Phœnician but also
to universal history, originated in a rising of the
commons against the ruling aristocratic houses.[3]
Mattan had left the royal power to be shared
by his son Pygmalion (or Pümeliun, according
to Lenormant), and a daughter, Elessar, several

---

[1] On the black obelisk in the British Museum. The
name is read there as Jahua son of Khumri, *i.e.,* Jehu son
of Omri ; on which see Dr. Hincks's note in Rawlinson's
Herodotus, i., pp. 378—380, and cp. Lenormant, ii., p. 185.

[2] So in Etym. Magn., s. v. Dido, quoted by Movers ;
cp. pp. 362—391.

[3] ii., 1, pp. 350—364.

. years his senior. But a popular *émeute*, for
which the disorders of many preceding years
had paved the way, deprived the princess of
all share in the government, and surrounded
the young king with democratic councillors.
Probably in order to strengthen her position
by the support· of the priestly party, Elessar
married Sicharbaal,[1] the high-priest of Melkarth,
brother of the late king, and chief functionary
of the national religion. His position not only
brought him in much revenue, but also gave
him rank next to the king, and made him,
during the minority of the latter, his legal representative.[2] To rid himself of so formidable
a rival, Pygmalion, as soon as he had grown to
manhood, caused him to be assassinated. His
widow, burning for revenge, formed a conspiracy
among the nobles to dethrone her brother, and
restore the aristocratic constitution ; and the
failure of this led to the flight of Elessar, accompanied by numerous nobles and their adherents. It seems to have been only after her
arrival in Libya that she received the name of
Dido, "the fugitive." The confusion that sprang

[1] Cp. Movers, note 67.
[2] See Movers, ii., 1, pp. 543—545.

up afterwards between the queen so denoted
by reason of her exile, and the moon-goddess
Astarte, who bore the epithet, as the wanderer
in the heavens,[1] is very curious as affording
an instance of one of the most fertile sources
of mythology, but does not bear directly upon
our present subject. What is of importance
for us to notice is that Tyre must have been
so weakened by this long period of disorder,
followed by the loss of many of its wealthiest
citizens, as to have little wish or power to in-
terfere in the concerns of its neighbours. Its
influence during this period was mainly felt
in the extension of the worship of Baal by
Athaliah, the wicked daughter of a wicked
Tyrian mother, Jezebel; and the dangers which
threatened the northern kingdom came from the
east, not from the west, from the kingdoms of
Damascus and Nineveh, bitterly hostile to each

---

[1] Compare the lines of Shelley—

> Art thou pale for weariness
> Of climbing heaven, and gazing on the earth,
> Wandering companionless
> Among the stars that have a different birth ?

The Etym. Magn., s. v. Dido, explains Διδώ by πλανῆτις, and
Movers identifies דִּידָא with נְדִידָא "die Umherir-
rende," p. 363, note 92. See also Kurts' Mythologie, p. 62.

other, but each alternately laying a heavy hand
of oppression on the kingdoms of Israel. The
only references that we have to Phœnicia during
this period are found in one of the two great
prophets of the northern kingdom, Amos.   He
threatens that "the Lord will send a fire into
the wall of Tyre, and it shall devour her
palaces, for three transgressions and for four,
because they delivered up an entire captivity
unto Edom, and remembered not the covenant
of brethren."[1] This seems to refer to the raids
of small bodies of slave-hunters, rather than to
any collective action on the part of the nation.
The yet earlier prophet of the southern kingdom, Joel, represents these bands as penetrating
even into the land of Judah, and selling "the
sons of Judah and the sons of Jerusalem to
the sons of Javan, that they might be removed
far from their own border."[2] And Homer gives
us some vivid pictures of their treachery and
cunning in kidnapping the children of the
Greek chieftains,[3] and carrying them beyond
the sea for sale.   The Edomites, like the

---

[1] i., p. 9.   [2] iii., p. 6.

[3] Odyss., xiv. 287, 298 ; xv. 415—429. "While pro-
fessedly describing an uncertified past, his combinations

Midianites of the days of Joseph, were the carriers of the desert, and "the children of Javan," or Grecians, as the authorized version rightly calls them, had by this time established most extensive commercial dealings with the Phœnicians.

We are surprised to find how quickly Tyre recovered from the loss inflicted upon her by the flight of the founders of Carthage. As in all the Greek tyrannies, which sprang up for the most part shortly after the period now under consideration, we find that the attempt of the Tyrian commons to shake off the rule of the few, only resulted in establishing the despotic rule of one.[1] But, as in Athens under the Peisistratids, Corinth under the Cypselids, Sicyon under Cleisthenes, Argos under Pheidon, this despotism was far from checking the prosperity of the state. The only direct effect of it which we can trace with clearness is the disaffection that it seems to have produced in the other cities of the Phœnician league. We find that in the great trouble that was soon to come upon

are involuntarily borrowed from the surrounding present."
—Grote, i., p. 454.

[1] Lenormant, ii., p. 187.

Tyre, few if any of its subject towns stood by
it, but all hastened to make submission to the
invader. This was Sargon, the father of
Sennacherib. There is reason to believe that
he was a usurper, and the founder of a new
and vigorous dynasty.[1] On his inscriptions he
claims the honour of the capture of Samaria,
and the completion of the captivity of Israel.
From other sources we learn that he made a
determined attack upon Phœnicia, which was
indeed the natural result of his possession of
Damascus. During the earlier years of the
Assyrian empire, its monarchs had been contented in the main with conducting their
commerce with the west through the agency
of the desert tribes, who served as carriers
for the Phœnicians. But the absorption of
the Chaldæans had given a more purely
military and aggressive character to the kingdom of Nineveh.[2] The kingdom of Damascus,
which, itself a dangerous neighbour to the
maritime states, had still served as their advanced guard against the Assyrians, had been
greatly weakened by the victories of Joash and

[1] Rawlinson's Herodotus, i., p. 385.
[2] Cp. Kenrick, p. 372, and Movers, ii., 1, p. 376, *sqq.*

Jeroboam II.; and finally fell an easy prey
to "the Tiger Lord of Asshur" (Tiglath-
Pileser), who captured Damascus, and slew the
last of its monarchs, Rezin. A firm alliance
between Syria, the two Jewish kingdoms, and
Phœnicia, might possibly have interposed an
effectual barrier to the growth of Assyria,[1] but
divided by mutual jealousies, they were power-
less to resist the conqueror's march.[2] The
trans-Jordanic tribes were swept into captivity;
the successor of the Tiger-king again attacked
the land of Israel,[3] and either he or the monarch
who seems to have supplanted him completed
the ruin of the northern kingdom. The narrative in the Book of Kings leaves us with

[1] Movers has shown reason for believing that *within*
the kingdom of Israel there was a strong party in favour of
Assyria (ii., 1, p. 378), which the monarchs of that country
fostered in accordance with their policy at that time.

[2] We find only one instance of any attempt to form
such a league. Towards the close of the reign of Tiglath-
Pileser, Mutton, king of Tyre, made an alliance with
Pekah, and they both refused to pay tribute to Assyria.
But an army was sent to enforce obedience. Hoshea
formed a conspiracy, slew Pekah, and then made terms
himself with Assyria, and Mutton finding himself de-
serted, was obliged to follow his example.—See Lenormant,
i., 391 (cp. p. 172, where there is a more doubtful instance
of the same kind).

[3] Lenormant, i., p. 392. Cp. p. 175.

the impression that it was Shalmaneser who captured the city of Samaria; but this is not directly asserted, and his successor, Sargon, claims the exploit for himself in one of the Khorsabad inscriptions. It seems most probable that the latter was Tartan, or commander-in-chief of the Assyrian army; and that the blockade of Samaria was commenced by Shalmaneser; but that on his death, either after he had returned to Assyria, or else in the land of Israel, or perhaps even in consequence of a rebellion at home occasioned by the long absence of the monarch from the capital,[1] Sargon succeeded in establishing himself on the throne. It is certainly to him that we must ascribe the important campaigns that followed. The inscription already referred to recounts, probably with truth, numerous other conquests which followed that of Samaria, all marked by the same extensive deportations of the conquered nations.[2] But in one case the monumental record is incomplete, or rather false. After describing the battle of Raphia, in which

Rawlinson's Herodotus, i., p. 387.

[2] For the objects of this policy see Ewald's good remarks, iii., pp. 302, 303.

the king of Gaza, and *Shebek*,[1] king of Egypt, were routed, and compelled to promise " tribute of gold, spices, horses, and camels," Sargon goes on to say : " Master of battles I crossed the sea of Jamnia in ships, like a fish. I annexed Kui and Tyre." The annals of Tyre, preserved by Josephus (Ant. IX., 14, 2), give a very different and probably truer story.[2] " Elulæus, to whom they gave the name Pya, ruled for thirty-six years. Upon the revolt of the Kittians,[3] he sailed against them, and reduced them to submission. Shalmaneser, having sent an army against these people, overran the whole of Phœnicia, and then, having made peace with all, returned home. But Sidon, and Ake, and Palæ-Tyrus, and many other cities, revolted from the Tyrians, and gave themselves up to the king of Assyria. Then, as the Tyrians had not submitted to him, the king marched against them again, and the Phœnicians contributed a fleet of sixty ships and eight hundred row-boats (ἐπικώπους). But the Tyrians sailing

---

[1] *So*, according to the Masoretic pointing in 2 Kings xvii. 4, but cp. Ewald, iii., 316, note 1. (First German edition.)

[2] Cp. Movers, ii., 1, pp. 383—385.

[3] Chittim, of Cyprus.

against these with twelve ships, scattered the
enemy's fleet; and took about five hundred
prisoners, and all in Tyre won much honour by
this. So the king of Assyria returned home,
after posting guards at the river [apparently
the copious spring of Ras-el-Ain, praised so
by Nonnus, xl. 360][1] and the aqueducts, to prevent the Tyrians from drawing water. But the
Tyrians held out for five years, and got their
water from wells that they dug."[2] Here, as perhaps in the Jewish annals, Shalmaneser is con-
fused with Sargon ; but this furnishes no ground
for speaking of the account as " probably unhis-
torical."[3]   Movers has well pointed out the importance of Cyprus (probably an old possession
of the Assyrians in their earlier palmy days),[4]
not only from its great productiveness, but also
as the only station for a fleet, intended to operate
against Phœnicia and Egypt, which would be
accessible to the Assyrian monarchs. It is probable, therefore, that the revolt of Cyprus against

[1] Kenrick, p. 346.
[2] Translated from the original, cp. Movers, *l. c.* The
version by Lenormant is not very correct (i., p. 396). Cp.
Cheyne's Isaiah, p. 91.
[3] Rawlinson, *u. s.*, p. 386, note 4.
[4] See Movers, ii., 1, p. 292.

the Tyrian rule was the work of Assyrian policy,
and was supported by Assyrian arms. The
appeal to the monarchy of Nineveh at this time
has a parallel in the appeal to the king of Persia
afterwards when the island seemed in the way
to become a powerful Greek kingdom under
Evagoras.[1] The connection of this campaign
with the battle of Raphia will readily be understood if we remember that to Egypt the Israelites, the Phœnicians, and the Philistines all were
looking as their ally against the threatening
domination of Assyria. It was the discovery of
a conspiracy of Hoshea with Seveh, or Shebek,
king of Egypt, that led to the complete captivity
of the northern kingdom ; and the prophets of
the period have constant references to the connection of interests and (intermittingly) of action
between the various objects of the ambition of
Assyria. The earlier Zechariah, in words already
quoted, speaks of the alarm that should fall upon
Askelon and Ashdod at hearing of the fate of
Tyre ; and Isaiah in several passages speaks of
Egypt as the hope of Phœnicia, though he does not
fail to point out how untrustworthy this hope was.[2]

[1] Grote, vii., pp. 17—20 (8 vol. ed.)
[2] Is. xx. 5, 6, xxiii. 5. Cp. Ewald, iii., p. 316; Movers, ii.,
I, p. 394, *sq.*

The result of this blockade of the island-city
of Tyre is not stated definitely by any authority,
for the Khorsabad inscription may refer only to
Palæ-Tyrus. But Movers[1] supplies some very
strong arguments for believing that the reduction
of the city was at last effected, not the least
forcible of which is the very suspicious silence of
the fragment of Menander (ap. Josephum[2]) as to
the final issue. The capture of some five hundred prisoners would hardly have been dwelt
upon so much if it had been cast into the shade
by a five years' successful defiance of the whole
power of Assyria. It is only one of the sadly
numerous instances in which M. Lenormant turns
unsupported conjectures into unqualified asser-
tions,[3] if he writes, "the siege lasted five years ;
and at last the lieutenants of Sargon, tired of
their useless efforts, and seeing no probable end

[1] ii., 1, p. 397—400.
[2] Antiq., ix., 14, 2. Mr. Cheyne draws just the opposite
conclusion from the language of Menander (Isaiah, p. 56);
but this is alike less natural in itself, and opposed to the
many other indications of the result. Sargon, in one of
his inscriptions now in the British Museum, distinctly
says that he "has destroyed the city of Tyre." Cp.
Cheyne's Isaiah, p. 239.
[3] Cp. Edinburgh Review for July, 1870.

to their undertaking, decided on raising the siege."[1] And again : "At the end of this long and fruitless siege, the Assyrians were compelled to retreat."[2] There seems, however, reason for believing that the terms conceded were honourable, and that Tyre was left in a condition of wealth and prosperity.[3]

Now we have again a long period of darkness, all authorities failing us, with the exception of the cuneiform inscriptions, which here and there shed some gleams of light upon the position of the Phœnician cities in relation to Assyria. Movers, writing before any of these records were deciphered, represents the century which elapsed between the siege of Tyre by Sargon's generals, and its capture by Nebuchadnezzar, as one of peaceful submission on their part to the Ninevite empire.[4] The evident desire of the Assyrian monarchs to bind together the various provinces that owned their sway by the ties of commerce and friendly intercourse, and to weld them into a compact and united kingdom, leads us to imagine that they would have furnished every

---

[1] ii., p. 190. [3] Kenrick, p. 380.
[2] i., p. 396. [4] ii., 1, pp. 400—402.

protection to the lucrative trade of Tyre. And that this was the case in the main is evident from the great prosperity which the city enjoyed during this period. We have a vivid picture of this in the words of the contemporary prophet Isaiah (xxiii. 7):

> Who hath decreed this against Tyre,
> The city that dispensed crowns,
> Whose merchants were princes,
> Whose traffickers the honoured of the land?

And a magnificent description of the same city, under the emblem of a ship, its wealth, strength, and luxury being symbolized by the beauty and firm structure of one of its own state galleys, is furnished to us by the somewhat later prophet Ezekiel.[1] But in spite of the great material advantages resulting from a close connection with Assyria (counterbalanced, however, to a certain extent by losses arising from the interruption of trade with countries at war with Assyria, and from the establishment of Assyrian colonies),[2] the attractions of the old alliance with Egypt, and the impatience of foreign rule, break-

[1] Chap. xxvii., of which an excellent translation is given by Kenrick, pp. 192—195.

[2] Movers, ii., 1, pp. 409—412.

ing out occasionally with unexpected fierceness
in the Phœnician race, sometimes shook their
fidelity. We find, for instance, that upon the
death of Sargon, Elulæus, the king of Tyre
mentioned before, profited by the temporary
confusion that ensued to extend his rule over
the other Phœnician cities, and to throw off the
yoke of Assyria. The first campaign of Sennacherib was directed against the rebel monarch,
and seems to have resulted in his expulsion, after
the capture of his capital.[1] The next instance of
resistance was offered by Sidon,[2] during the disturbances which followed the assassination of
Sennacherib; but his successor, Esarhaddon,
marched in person into Phœnicia, and quelled
the revolt. He says himself of Sidon, in an inscription: "I have put all its grandees to death;
I destroyed its walls and its houses; I threw
them into the sea; I destroyed the sites of its
temples."[3]

Not twenty years after this,[4] we find the Phœnicians again in revolt, this time supported by
the Ethiopian king of Egypt, who succeeded
Tirhakah; but the Assyrian monarch, Asshur-

---

[1] Lenormant, ii., p. 191.　　[3] Lenormant, ii., p. 192.
[2] Rawlinson, i., p. 390.　　[4] Rawlinson, i., p. 395.

banipal, after a successful campaign in Egypt, reduced them again to submission.

The great Scythic invasion of B.C. 620 (circ.) seems to have had but little permanent effect upon any of the nations over which it swept like a whirlwind. But the revival of Egyptian power under Psammetichus, and the capture and de-struction of Nineveh by the Medes and Baby-lonians, were far more fruitful of results.[1] When Necho, the son of Psammetichus, advanced into Syria to share the spoils of the Ninevite empire, the Phœnician cities seem to have welcomed him with alacrity, and aided him with their fleet in his probably successful attempt to circum-navigate Africa. Josiah, faithful to his Babylo-nian allies, in vain endeavoured to stop the course of the invader at Megiddo, and was slain in battle there; but the Egyptian army suffered a complete defeat at Carchemish, at the hands of Nebuchadnezzar. Syria was utterly lost to the Pharaohs, and when afterwards the kings of Egypt attempted to protect their frontier by securing the alliance of the kings of Judah, they only brought ruin on their allies. At the time of the capture of Jerusalem, in the reign of

[1] Ewald, iii., p. 424, *sq.*

Jehoiakim,[1] and again when it suffered the same
fate under Jehoiachin, Nebuchadnezzar seems to
have had no leisure to turn his arms against
Phœnicia, and its citizens began to feel themselves secure.[2]   But Ezekiel warned them in
words of eloquent denunciation of the desolation that should soon come upon them : " Because
that Tyrus hath said against Jerusalem, Aha, she
is broken that was the gates of the nations : I
shall be replenished, now she is laid waste : therefore thus saith the Lord God, Behold I am
against thee, O Tyrus, and will cause many
nations to come up against thee, as the sea
causeth his waves to come up. And they shall
destroy the walls of Tyrus, and break down her
towers." The prophecy was soon, at least in
spirit, to be fulfilled. It was probably after the
capture of Jerusalem that Nebuchadnezzar

[1] See, however, Stanley, " Jewish Church," ii., p. 539.
[2] There seems even to have been at this time some
alliance between Phœnicia and the Chaldeans. At least
Apries (Pharaoh Hophra) is said to have taken Sidon by
storm, and fought a naval battle with the Tyrians (Herod.,
ii., p. 161). Perhaps they changed sides after the battle of
Carchemish, or at least were neutral. Lenormant however places this invasion of Uahprahet (as he calls him)
after the capture of Tyre. But see Sir J. G. Wilkinson's
note in Rawlinson's Herodotus, *l. c.*

marched against the Phœnician cities, which seem (willingly or by compulsion) to have joined the coalition of Zedekiah and Pharaoh Hophra, with the Moabites, the Ammonites, and the Edomites, against the Babylonian conqueror.[1] Tyre was the only one which offered any lasting resistance, and against this the full force of Nebuchadnezzar was directed. The thirteen years' siege that ensued was one of the most famous in history; but, as in the case of the leaguer of Sargon, we are quite unable to speak with confidence as to its termination. It has usually been supposed that Tyre was taken and destroyed; but this supposition rests upon the assumption that the prophecies of Ezekiel must have had a complete and exact fulfilment. The instance of Jonah at Nineveh shows us that this need not have been so, and other words of the prophet, spoken sixteen years after his first denunciations, seem to imply that the fate which he had threatened did not actually fall upon Tyre.

[1] See last note on the preceding page; cp. Movers, ii., I, pp. 426 and 450—458.

[2] Ezek. xxix. 17. Cp. Kenrick, pp. 388—390, and Dict. Bible, s.v. Tyre. Hitzig on Ezek. xxvi. denies that the prophecy was ever fulfilled. Fairbairn naturally takes the opposite view.

Movers has discussed the question with his usual exhaustive completeness (ii. 1. 427—449), and comes to the conclusion that the city finally submitted, but on honourable conditions, and that at any rate the island-city was never captured by force. Be this as it may, the long duration of the siege must have inflicted a serious blow upon the prosperity of Tyre; and though we find a series of kings filling the throne down to the days of Alexander, they were little more than satraps of the kings of Babylon, and afterwards of Persia. The independent national life of the Phœnician cities terminated with their absorption into the empire of Nebuchadnezzar. The same limit may be assigned for the purposes of the present essay to the national life of the children of Israel; and here we may close this rapid survey of the exterior history of the mutual relations of the two great peoples of Palestine. The following chapters will contain a consideration of the results, political, social, and religious, of these relations.

CHAPTER III.

THE INFLUENCE OF PHŒNICIA UPON ISRAEL, POLITICAL AND SOCIAL.

Common Race Characteristics—For the most part lost—
Canaanite and Phœnician Influence tending in the same
direction—Counteracting Influences—Vows—Civic Leagues—
Literature—Manufactures—Phœnician carrying Trade—Direct
Commerce.

" THE earliest period of antiquity was an age
when nations were not crowded together
in large loose masses, but lived one beside the
other, like so many families, each retaining its
own sharply defined character and distinct culture ; and when even the smallest tribe shut itself
up in its own individuality, and relied solely on
its own resources to attain whatever appeared to
be its highest good. . . . Just as Athens and
Rome, with the smallest possible territory, could
gain a place in the history of the world, so also
could a nation of Palestine. Now two nations
of Palestine, we know, above all others that met

there, bore away this palm,—two nations so different that it is hard to imagine a stronger contrast, and even acting upon each other in virtue of this very contrast to intensify their divergence, yet both of them so constituted that the result of their endeavours became permanent, and among the most conspicuous fruits of the world's history."[1]

Before we attempt to determine the nature and results of their action on each other, two stumbling-blocks must be removed that present themselves at the very commencement of our path. The Israelites, as we have already seen, probably belonged to the same great stock, if not to the same division of it, as the Phœnicians; and for centuries they had within their borders the remnants of conquered tribes that had the closest affinity to the population of the maritime cities. If then we find any points of resemblance to the latter in the political, social, and religious conditions of the former, we shall have to attempt the preliminary inquiry how far these are due to the inherent tendencies of the Semitic stock, and how far they may be ascribed to the internal action of the Canaanite tribes ; and it is only

[1] Ewald, i., pp. 223, 234.

that which still remains unaccounted for by the action of these constant, and, so to speak, primary influences, that can fairly be traced to the conscious or unconscious agency of the Phœnicians. The first of these questions admits the more readily of at least partial solution, but in both we shall probably have to content ourselves with an approximation to the truth.

The evidence of language, here apparently incontestable, proves that the Phœnicians belonged to the Semitic stock,[1] but the historian is fairly puzzled to find the prevalent Semitic characteristics entirely wanting among the Phœnicians. "The proper characteristic of the Semites is to have no industry, no political spirit, no municipal organization; navigation and colonization seem distasteful to them; their action confined itself to the East, and entered into the current of the affairs of Europe only indirectly. In Phœnicia, on the contrary, we find an industrial civilization, political revolutions, the most active commerce that was known to antiquity, a nation incessantly penetrating in all directions into the outer world, and mingled in all the destinies of the Mediterranean nations.

[1] See above, p. 10.

In religion there is the same contrast : instead of
the severe monotheism, the lofty conception of
the Deity, the pure ritual which characterizes
the Semitic nations, we find among the Phœnicians a coarse mythology, base and ignoble
gods, voluptuousness raised to an act of religion.
The most sensual myths of antiquity, the
phallic rites, the trade in prostitutes, the infa-
mous institutions of the Galli and the ἱερόδουλοι
come in great measure from Phœnicia. Perhaps
if we had to point out among all the nations of
antiquity those whose physiognomy contrasted
most with that of the Semites, we should be
tempted to name the Phœnicians. And yet
this is the nation which linguistic facts prove to
have been in the closest fraternity with the
Hebrews."[1] The only solution of this enigma is
to suppose that the Phœnicians, separating
early from the general stock, and rapidly developing a luxurious commercial life, abandoned
their primitive character, but not their language,
and so became soon very distinct from and
almost the opposite of their nomadic brethren.[2]

---

[1] Rénan, "Histoire des Langues Semitiques," pp. 183,
184.

[2] This is of course directly opposed to the theory of

M. Rénan reminds us of the marvellous change
which, with all its narrow and exclusive patriotism, has passed over the Jewish nation ; and
tells us that the baseness and the degradation of the Arab who pursues commerce and
handicrafts in the towns of Barbary furnishes a
striking contrast to the natural pride of the true
Arab, the Arab of the desert.[2] Benedict Spinoza,
Moses Mendelssohn, and Heinrich Heine are
alone enough to show how little race characteristics can be regarded as immutable. We may
therefore. assume with confidence that all or
nearly all the points of resemblance between the
Phœnicians and Israelites in their primeval home
had become obliterated in the course of the
centuries which had witnessed them living such
diverse lives.

It is much less easy to determine the effect
that the Canaanitish kinsmen of the Phœnicians had in producing after the arrival of the

Prof. Rawlinson, that the Phœnicians did not come into
the land about Tyre and Sidon till long after the entrance
of the children of Israel on the Promised Land ; but we
have seen already that this view is supported by no competent authorities, and very few noteworthy arguments.

[2] Rénan has well brought out the effects of a nomadic
life, p. 498.

Israelites some degree of assimilation. These Canaanites were very far from being a barbarous nation; on the contrary, we have many indications that they had already attained to a high but terribly corrupt civilization,—"a sort of over-ripeness in their beautiful land, which may probably have been largely due to their never-ceasing divisions, through which every petty town could manufacture its own laws,—the worse, the better."[1] The fresh energy of the invading hosts, their consciousness of a divine guidance, and, we need not fear to add, the direct assistance of Jahveh (vouchsafed to the chosen people), carried the Israelites victorious through the first great battles of the war. But though they established themselves firmly in the strongholds of the hill country, "walking," as their poets loved to express it, "on the high places of the land,"[2] the fertile valleys remained to a large extent in the hands of the Canaanites, and the settlements of the Israelites were often "like islands shaken by a stormy ocean."[3] As soon as the firm controlling hand of Joshua was removed,

[1] Ewald, i., p. 241.
[2] See references in Ewald, ii., p. 264.
[3] Ewald, *ibid.*

the invaders became at once disorganized and
disunited, and to the isolated communities the
neighbourhood of the luxurious and cultured
Canaanites must have furnished constant sources
of attraction and temptation. The story of the
sin of Achan gives us just a glimpse into the
wealth which, even thus early, traffic with the
East must have brought into the land ; and
there are not wanting indications of manufacturing industry. The "prey of diverse colours,"
which the mother of Sisera is represented as
anticipating, may well have been the product of
the looms of the conquered Canaanites. We
must certainly ascribe to their influence, and not
to that of the Phœnicians, during this early
period at any rate, the constant lapses from the
worship of Jahveh into the foul and idolatrous
cult of Baal and Ashtaroth. The simple words
of the Book of Judges bring this forcibly before
us : "And the children of Israel dwelt among
the Canaanites, Hittites, and Amorites, and
Perizzites, and Hivites, and Jebusites : and they
took their daughters to be their wives, and gave
their daughters to their sons, and served their
gods. And the children of Israel did evil in the
sight of the Lord, and forgat the Lord their

God, and served Baalim and the groves" (Ashtaroth).[1] Yet, in the midst of all the effeminate
vice that is implied in these words, the character
of the Jewish nation seems to have retained much
of its primitive simplicity. We must never forget
that the dangerous attractions of the Canaanites
were counterbalanced to a certain extent by the
bitter hostility that must have lain beneath temporary alliances and connexions, and that there
were rarely wanting some faithful adherents of
Jahveh to call the people back to their alle-
giance to the God of their fathers.[2] A victory
like that of Deborah and Barak must have
swept away the results of years of treacherously
peaceful intercourse. And on the whole the
impression that we derive from the chronicle of
this period is that of primitive simplicity rather
than luxurious civilization. "The disorders of
the time breathe always the air rather of the
desert than of the city."[3] Many little phrases
still in use remind us of the nomadic life of the
desert ;[4] and the story of Ruth, as "she stood

[1] Judges iii. 5—7.
[2] Compare the story of the overthrow of the altar of
Baal in Ophrah, by Gideon.
[3] Stanley, "Jewish Church," i., p. 294.
[4] Cp. Stanley, *u. s.*, p. 295.

in tears amid the alien corn," is full of a delicious pastoral freshness.[1] The whole constitution of Joshua was directed to the establishment and maintenance of the bulk of the nation in the condition of small yeomen farmers ;[2] and any one who has studied with care the internal history of the Roman Republic[3] will understand the vital importance of his salutary regulations as to the tenure of land to the strength and stability of the nation. In spite of the many temptations from the Canaanites, it was possible to preserve, at least in the parts of the country furthest removed from the corrupting atmosphere of the larger towns, a national life fundamentally pure and wholesome. This might have been attained in a far higher degree if the Divine commands had been faithfully executed, the Canaanites rooted out, and each free citizen placed in possession of his share of the fertile territory. Even as it was, this period had its gleams of light breaking through the dark-

Cp. Ewald, i., p. 154 ; ii., p. 320.

[2] Cp. especially Milman, "History of the Jews," i., pp. 161 and 230—233.

[3] The land-question at Rome is admirably discussed by Ihne, "Römische Geschichte," vol. i., book ii., cc. 7 and 17 ; book iii., c. 3.

ness, or perhaps we should rather say that if we could penetrate the veil that too much hides it from us, we should find that what is covered is far less gloomy than we might have imagined. We need not follow Ewald in his somewhat arbitrary and dogmatic assignment of the Biblical narrative to various authors, whose dates and tendencies he fixes with so much confidence.[1] But we may be willing to admit that the main object of the compiler of the Book of Judges was to point out the evils that resulted from anarchy, and from a desertion of the one true God, and that he passed over all that would not tend to impress this the more deeply on the minds of his readers.[2]

The veil is lifted for us once; and though the view that we get then shows us the life of Northern Israel at a somewhat later time than that which we are now considering, we may well

[1] Cp. i., pp. 159—163.

[2] It is hard to see the force of Ewald's arguments for assigning the work to two early authorities and a later *rédacteur*. There is nothing unnatural, it seems to me, in supposing that the same writer, living in the reign of one of the good kings, wished to exalt both the advantages of monarchy, and the blessings that accompanied fidelity to Jahveh.

believe that for our present purpose it may be taken as a faithful representation of the condition of things at an earlier period. The beautiful " Song of Solomon" is probably but little later than the days of the great monarch whose name it bears, for this idyllic drama must have been composed before Tirzah had ceased to be a capital city almost rivalling Jerusalem.[1] It breathes throughout a spirit of reaction against the splendour of the court of Solomon, and the polygamy that threatened to corrupt the simple domestic life of the people. While on the one hand it points to a condition of no small literary development, on the other hand it is fragrant with the freshness and innocence of rustic life, contrasted sharply with the luxury and effeminacy of the city and the palace. We cannot believe that the picture of the fairest among women that went her way forth by the footsteps of the flock, and fed her kids beside the shepherds' tents, is drawn entirely from the fancy of the poet. In all the temptations to vice that abounded in the groves of Ashtaroth, there must have been many a fresh and simple heart,

[1] See Ewald, iii., pp. 173—175. Rénan assigns it to the lifetime of Solomon. See the Preface to his translation.

that murmured to itself, " My dove, my unde-
filed is one, she the one of her mother, she the
choice of her that bare her."[1]

The surest test of the moral elevation of an
age we find in reverence for women,[2] and if we
find them, even in the more corrupt and disorganized tribes of Northern Canaan, distributing
the spoil in the rejoicings after victory,[3] and in
general enjoying unusual freedom and respect,
we cannot believe that the heart of the nation
can have been deeply tainted. We find indeed
outbursts of. licentious passion, resulting in
horrible outrage, but the words with which such
deeds were spoken of, " such folly should not be
wrought in Israel," point to a national life still
sound and morally awake.[4]

Two points dwelt upon by Dean Stanley as
instances of Phœnician influence would seem to
be more justly ascribed to the intercourse with

[1] Çant. vi. 9.

[2] We cannot fail to remember how Tacitus loves to
bring this out in his contrast of the fresh Teutonic tribes
with his own fast-sinking country. Compare, too, the
Penelope and Nausicaa of Homer with Pericles' idea oi
woman, and the wife of Xenophon's Œconomicus.

[3] Judges v. 11 ; Ps. lxviii. 11. *sq.*; Is. ix. 5 (from Ewald,
ii., p. 355).

[4] Cp. Ewald, ii., p. 351, with refefences in note 2.

the Canaanites. The first is the tendency to
the frequent use of vows. "The impulse from
his early oath, which nerved the courage and
patriotism of Hannibal from childhood to age in
his warfare against Rome, may fitly be taken
as an illustration of the feeling which, in its
highest and noblest forms, led to the consecration of Samson and Samuel, and in its unautho-
rized excesses to the rash vows of the whole
nation against the tribe of Benjamin, of Jephthah against his daughter, of Saul against
Jonathan. These spasmodic efforts after self-
restraint are precisely what we should expect in
an age which had no other mode of steadying
its purposes amidst the general anarchy in which
it was enveloped, and accordingly in that age
they first appear, and within its limits expire."[1]
But it must not escape our notice that all the
instances here adduced are drawn from the very
tribes that must have been exposed the least
to purely Phœnician influences. It is going
far from the most immediate and potent cause
to trace such influence in the case of the trans-
Jordanic Jephthah. The striking parallel of
Hannibal's oath only tends to confirm our

[1] Jewish Church, i., p. 294.

belief in the fundamental identity of the Canaanites and the Phœnicians, and not to induce us
to ascribe to the latter what may well be traced
to the former. Similar reasoning seems to hold
good as regards Dean Stanley's second instance.
Ewald rightly lays much stress upon the change
from a purely tribal constitution to a confederate
civic life, such as that displayed by the league
that placed itself under the protection of Baal-
Berith, the "Covenant God."[1] But when he says
that the example of such civic life and civic
leagues was obviously given to the northern
regions by their Phœnician neighbours, and by
the ancient Canaanite customs, we may fairly
ask what need there is to assume the agency of
the former, when the influence of the latter was
of itself adequate to produce the results. Indeed
there are indications in the account of the league
of Baal-Berith, of which Shechem was the centre, to show that it was at least semi-Canaanite
in its composition.

On the other hand, we may fairly ascribe to
more direct Phœnician influence the development of art and of literature among the Israel-

---

[1] Ewald, ii., pp. 341—344. Cp. Judges viii. 33, and
Stanley, i., pp. 293 and 352.

ites of the time of the Judges. The origin of writing, and the date of its first employment, are subjects which have been much debated, and the paucity of evidence makes it probable that we shall never be able to arrive at any posi-. tive conclusion. " L'ignorance où nous sommes des vrais rapports des Hébreux d'une part avec les Hyksos, et de l'autre avec les Phéniciens d'une époque reculée, est ici, comme sur une foule de points, la source de grandes perplexités."[1] But the opinion of the best authorities appears to be that writing was unknown to the Israelites before their descent into the land of Egypt ; that from some source (probably wholly unconnected with hieroglyphics) they acquired it there, but that it did not come into general use till after they had settled in the land of Canaan.[2] At any rate it is certain that a vigorous popular literature was developed during the time of the Judges. There are not only many historical fragments which the most unsparing criticism is compelled to ascribe to this era, but we also find lyrics which unite the greatest boldness and animation with a finished artistic structure. To

[1] Rénan, Histoire, p. 118. See above, pp. 41—43.
[2] Cp. Rénan, pp. 112—118; Ewald, i., 45—53 ; ii., 19—21.

take the most striking instance, the Song of
Deborah:[1] " The solemn religious commencement
—the picturesque description of the state of the
country—the mustering of the troops from all
quarters—the sudden transition to the most
contemptuous sarcasm against the tribes that
stood aloof—the life, fire, and energy of the
battle—the bitter pathos of the close,"[2] combine
to make it all but unrivalled in the literature of
any nation. The moral elevation, and the firm
reliance on the protection of Jahveh, the confidence in the final overthrow of His enemies,
must have been drawn from the heart of the
Chosen People, where there lay deep down
something better than the Arab's love of wild-
ness and isolation, something better than the
Phœnician's greed of gain.[3] But the perfection
of the form in the midst of the archaic simplicity
of tone may surely have owed something to the
influence of the civilized neighbouring nation,
that even then seems to have possessed a

---

[1] " Le cantique de Débora, dont l'authenticité a enlevé
les suffrages des critiques les plus difficiles." — Rénan,
p. 124.

[2] Milman, i., p. 246, where there is a beautiful rhyth-
mical translation given.

[3] Ewald, ii., p. 350.

copious literature.[1]　And "a people which on every higher occasion felt itself elevated by refined poetry, and in which songs full of art and wit, sung in alternate choirs by all who bore part in the solemnity, formed the real life and best consecration of a popular festival (and Deborah's songs are clearly of this kind), cannot be considered to stand upon any low level."[2]

It is not easy to determine the extent to which arts and manufactures were to be found among the Israelites at this period. Some among them, at any rate, had acquired no little skill in this respect during their residence in Egypt, for when we are told in the account of the construction of the tabernacle that "the Lord put wisdom and understanding in the heart of Bezaleel and Aholiab, and every wise-hearted man, to know how to work all manner of work for the service of the sanctuary," we are probably only to see in this an instance of

[1] The extent to which this argument may be pressed will of course depend upon the amount of adhesion which we give to the theories which would make Jacob's Blessing, and Miriam's Song of Triumph, the productions of a later age.　See Rénan, p. 124.

[2] Ewald, ii., p. 355.

the pious and true conception of the Hebrews, who saw in all artistic powers, however acquired, tokens of the favour of the Author of every good and perfect gift. On the other hand, we find that Solomon was obliged to fetch all the skilled workmen for the building of his temple from Phœnicia ; and this seems to point to a great decay rather than an advance in the industrial capacities of his own people. It is natural of course to suppose that the disturbed state of the country during the period of the Judges, and the repeated invasions and oppressions by foreign nations, should have produced this. But we may also attach much weight to the neighbourhood of the πολυδαίδαλοι Σιδώνιοι, as Homer calls them. When a highly civilized manufacturing nation is brought into contact with one of inferior social advancement, it not unfrequently happens that its influence on the native industry of the latter is all but fatal. We can readily conceive that those of the Israelites who retained some knowledge of the various processes of manufacture that they had learnt in Egypt, would find themselves driven from the markets of their own towns and villages by the superior artistic excellence, and possibly greater cheap-

ness (the result of slave labour), of the goods
that were brought in constantly by the Phœnician hucksters.[1] They would thus naturally betake themselves to agriculture, thereby making
their former rivals their eager customers, and
all knowledge of higher art-workmanship would
die out by degrees from among them. This
view is of course not inconsistent with the existence of a certain amount of domestic industry.
Of this we have evidence in the picture given us
in the Book of Proverbs of the virtuous woman
who "maketh fine linen and selleth it : she de-
livereth girdles to the Canaanite."[2] The use of
the Gentile name, found in Hosea and Isaiah
also, as a synonym for merchant or pedlar, may
arise from the identity of the Phœnicians and
the Canaanites ; but it seems more probable
that the ancient inhabitants of the country, deprived of all their land, had to betake themselves to petty trade as the only means of a
livelihood open to them.[3]

[1] On these see Kenrick, p. 232. More is said of them
below.

[2] See De Wette's version, xxxi. 24 ; xii. 7 ; xxiii. 8 ;
cp. Movers, ii., 3, p. 12, and Rénan, Histoire, etc.,
p. 183.

[3] Kenrick, p. 232.

Hitherto the problem of distinguishing between the influence of the Canaanites in the land, and the Phœnicians on its borders, has been difficult ; it may be, indeed, insoluble. But when we come to consider the results of commerce on a wider scale, we find ourselves on safer ground. Professor Rawlinson has called attention to the fact (already referred to) that " Scripture does not introduce to our notice the real artistic and commercial Tyrians and Sidonians till the reigns of David and Solomon." [1] But if we are not wrong in following something like a con- sensus of authorities, and in attributing the Phœnician settlements in Canaan to a period antecedent (and probably long antecedent) to the Israelitish conquest, their commerce must already have been very important. There is no doubt that the peace and prosperity of the land under David and Solomon must have greatly increased it ; and therefore in what remains to be said on this subject, the remarks made will apply especially to the period of the kings. But when we find the Phœnicians spoken of almost invariably by the ancients as the inventors of

---

[1] Herodotus, vol. iv., p. 202.

commerce,[1] when Herodotus (i. 1), represents the Phœnicians as bringing Egyptian and Assyrian wares to Greece in the very dawn of the mythological period, and when we find the cities of Northern Phœnicia, Byblus, Berytus, and Aradus sending out numerous colonies at a time which Movers[2] (perhaps too definitely) places before B.C. 1600, we cannot doubt that the Phœnician commerce was widely extended at the very commencement of the historic period. Just as their trade by sea had its origin in the fishing excursions to which Sidon owed its name,[3] so their trade by land would naturally arise from the need that they had of the agricultural products of the inland regions. But the petty trade that had these small beginnings soon developed into a far-reaching commerce. The fortunate position of Phœnicia, " the sole medium of communication between the Semitic race and the rest of the world,"[4] on the coast of the Mediterranean, soon brought it into close commercial relations with Egypt and Assyria.

[1] "Mercaturas invenerunt Poeni," Plin., vii., p. 57. See many more authorities in Movers, ii., 3, p. 14.

[2] ii., 3, p. 21.

[3] Movers, *u. s.*, p. 15.

[4] Rénan, p. 115.

The products of the former were perhaps the more immediately valuable, but the trade with the latter was indirectly the most extensive. For through its territories flowed in a ceaseless stream the riches of the remoter East, and the spices and precious stones of India had all to pass through Tyre or Sidon on their way to the western world. Movers rates so highly the value of this commerce in the earliest times, that he holds the trade of Sidon in the five centuries that preceded her capture by the Philistines, to have been equal to that of Tyre in its palmiest days.[1] It was carried on partly by means of colonies planted along the most frequented routes, partly by settlements of Phœnician traders in foreign towns,[2] but mainly, perhaps, by the travelling merchants, going from fair to fair, and forming caravans of asses and mules for their shorter journeys, but camels and dromedaries whenever they had to cross the desert.[3] These caravans were usually managed by the Arabs, so that the prophet was describing what he had seen already, in a measure, when he said of the

[1] ii., 3, p. 22.
[2] Movers, ii., 3, pp. 112—126.
[3] *Ibid.*, p. 128, and the Biblical references in note 3*a*.

future glory of Israel, "The stream of camels shall cover thee, the dromedaries of Midian and Ephah ; all they from Sheba shall come ; they shall bring gold and incense."[1] For their convenience, "highways in the desert" had been constructed at a very early period, and supplied with wells and caravanserais.[2] Now most, and sometimes all of these routes, passed through the land of the children of Israel ; and apart from the strong security for peace between the two people that was thus afforded, the direct advantages must have been very great. The Phœnician traders would gladly save themselves the burden of carrying provisions with them, until they reached the borders of the desert, and so both for their daily needs, and also, it is probable, for their stock for the desert journey, they would be dependent upon the Jewish peasant proprietors along their route. Where they could, of course they would pay in their

---

[1] Isa. lx. 6. The passage gains in force if we suppose (accepting the hypothesis of a later origin for Is. xl.—lxvi.) that the prophet was writing at Babylon, and describing one of the caravans that were constantly bringing the wealth of the desert thither. The country with which the historic Isaiah was especially familiar would lie somewhat out of the direct line of this commerce.

[2] Many references in Movers, ii., 3, p. 133.

own manufactured goods, but in many cases silver would be preferred.

The extent of the whole trade of Phœnicia with the Holy Land, including direct and immediate commerce, as well as this traffic, so to speak, *en passant*, may be guessed at by the comparative plenty of silver. Even in the time of Abraham it was far from uncommon, and its value does not seem to have been excessively high. It is the recognized currency: the patriarch buys a field for 400 shekels of silver, "current with the merchant;" and all the pecuniary penalties in the Mosaic law are assessed in the same way. Now when we remember that this was long before the age of barter had passed away in Greece or in Persia,[1] that silver is very much less widely distributed, and much more difficult to procure than gold, so that the only important' silver-mines known before the discovery of those at Laureum were the mines of Tarshish ; when we remember, further, that all the silver drawn from this source must have

[1] Perhaps I should rather have written Bactria, for the authority on which I speak is the absence of any mention of money in the Zend-Avesta. Cp. Movers, *u. s.*, and Schleicher's Indogermanische Chrestomathie, p. 119, and Compendium, p. 5.

passed through the hands of the Phœnicians, we may form some notion of the extent of the traffic with Canaan, which made silver not only the established, but also an abundant circulating medium.[1]

The direct trade of Phœnicia with Israel must have been very extensive. We have noticed already the immense importance of the produce of Palestine to the over-peopled Phœnician cities on the coast. Then, as in later times, "their country was nourished by the king's country."[2] Hence we naturally find that Ezekiel places first of the the articles of commerce, Minnith wheat,[3] and Panneg (possibly millet).[4] Indeed, the value of this trade was such that it seems to have been mainly in the hands of the kings,[5] who had large

[1] See Movers' very interesting discussion of this question, ii., 3, pp. 27—57.

[2] Acts xii. 20.

[3] "Judah and the land of Israel were thy merchants: wheat of Minnith and Panneg, grape-honey, and oil and balsam, they brought into thy markets." Movers thinks that Minnith-wheat had come to be used as a generic name for the finest kind. Cp. ii., 3, p. 209.

[4] See Kenrick, p. 194, note 6, and Dict. Bible, *in voc.*

[5] We may compare the care which the Roman emperors exercised over the corn-supply. The *præfectus annonæ* was one of the three most important officers in Rome. Cp. Tac. Ann., i., 7, with Orelli's note.

crown estates themselves in the plain of Sharon.[1]
The wheat and barley, oil and wine, which Solomon gave to the servants of Hiram, were but
specimens of the produce that was always flow-
ing from the one country into the other. In the
north of Palestine they were conveyed by asses,
the usual beasts of burden, along the great caravan roads; and in this branch of commerce,
remunerative, but sometimes attended with degrading subservience, the tribe of Issachar took
a leading part. "Issachar is a strong ass couching
down between two burdens, and he saw that rest
was good, and the land that it was pleasant;
and he bowed his shoulders to bear, and became
a servant unto tribute."[2] The southern district,
on the other hand, sent its produce to Joppa,
whence it was carried by sea to Tyre and Sidon.
The corn trade followed the same line for centuries; we find that even under the Romans the
Jews had to send their tribute through Joppa to
Sidon, where it was sold for the benefit of the

---

[1] Movers, ii., 3, p. 210; ii., 1, pp. 314 and 524.

[2] See above, p. 51; and cp. Movers, ii., 1, p. 309 *f*;
Ewald, ii., p. 327, who thinks that the same charge
might be brought against the other northern tribes, but
but that the etymology of the name Issachar (*he is a
hired servant*) caused him to be selected.

imperial exchequer. Movers by an elaborate calculation, which of course can give but an approximation to the truth, in the state of our knowledge on the subject, estimates the value of the wheat annually sold by the Jews in the market of Sidon at more than £2,000,000 sterling.[1] The trade in olive-oil was the special source of the wealth of southern Palestine, as the corn trade was to the northern tribes ; for " the whole hill country between the high ridges of mountains on which Jerusalem and Hebron lie, is the very country for the olive."[2]   But from its very abundance, and the comparatively small demand for it where it was produced, its price was low, and the chief portion of the profit must have been made by the Phœnicians, who sold it into foreign lands, where its reputation was high,[3] and especially to Egypt, where the native oil was bad. Phœnicia produced so much wine itself, that it would have little occasion to import any, so that this department of commerce

---

[1] Movers, ii., 3, p. 212*f.*
[2] Ritter, quoted by Movers, ii., 3, p. 215.
[3] Hosea xii. 1 ; Isaiah lvii. 9. But in the latter passage Mr. Cheyne supposes Baal to be the king to whom reference is made.

seems to have been of little importance.[1] On
the other hand, one of the most valuable exports
was *honey,*[2] under which term we must include
not only the produce of bees, but also date-
honey,[3] and a kind of inspissated grape-syrup,
which is still an export of Palestine, under the
name of *dibs*. Among the other articles of raw
produce which Phœnicia obtained from the
children of Israel were wool, flax, linen, and
the much-debated byssus. The wool came
naturally from the hill country of Gilead and
of Judah, while the flax was grown in abundance in Galilee. Both were of great importance for the Phœnicians, whose trade consisted so largely of dyed goods. But the raw
material generally did not pass into their hands
before it had been woven into fabrics of various
kinds, the Galilean women weaving linen espe-

---

1 Hitzig (referred to by Rénan, p. 207) has pointed out
the curious fact that the various words relating to wine
among the *Semites* are not Semitic. Nothing is less
likely than that οἶνος was borrowed from יין; but the reverse seems probable. See Dict. Bible, iii., p. 1775*a*. Cp.
Curtius, "Griechische Etymologie," p. 363.

2 דְּבַשׁ (Ezek. xxvii. 17).

3 Cp. Plin. xiii. 9, Movers, ii., 3, pp. 216 and 234, note
126, with Kenrick, p. 194, note 7.

cially, the women of Judah woollen cloth.[1] We
may remember how prominent a feature this
industry is made in the picture of the virtuous
woman given in the Book of Proverbs. That it
was highly profitable is shown by Movers from
a passage in the Mischna, which rates the weekly
earnings of a woman at from five to ten shekels
of silver. The linen of Palestine seems to have
been particularly famous ; at a later time we
find that which came from Scythopolis ranking
above all other known kinds. Byssus, which
was grown in Canaan from a very early age,
Movers holds to have been a kind of cotton,
gathered not from the cotton-tree, which was
not known till a later period, but from a species
of annual shrub.[2] Whatever it may have been,
it furnished another article of commerce for the
Phœnician traders. If we add to these products
dates, resin (the so-called balm of Gilead), styrax,
ladanum, asphalt, and, most precious of all, the

---

[1] Movers, ii., 3, pp. 216, 217.

[2] *u. s.*, pp. 218, 219. Cp. Sir J. G. Wilkinson's note to
Herod., ii., p. 86, note 6. " Byssus in its real sense was
cotton, but it was also a general term." On the other
hand, Mr. Yates (Textrinum Antiquorum, p. 276), and
Mr. W. A. Wright (Dict. Bible, ii. p. 123*a*), hold that it
was strictly fine linen.

true balsam, that was worth twice its own weight in silver, we shall have completed the list of the principal exports of the land of Israel.

Of her imports from Phœnicia we are able to form a less definite conception. The linen and woollen cloth woven by the women of Israel would doubtless be brought back to them dyed in the famous Tyrian purples; and articles of luxury of every kind would be carried from house to house by the Canaanitish pedlars already referred to. But there are only two important items of commerce on which we can speak with definiteness. In Jerusalem the Tyrians had established a trade in fish,[1] probably the salted tunnies of the Euxine, that were a favourite food at Athens, possibly even the pickled fish of Gades, which the Carthaginians valued so highly that in the days of their rule of Spain they forbade any to be exported, save to their own metropolis.[2] Besides this, we may be sure that it was from Phœnicia that the

[1] Nehemiah xiii. 16. On the Phœnician tunny-fisheries there is much information collected in Nilsson's "Die Ureinwohner des Scandinavischen Nordens," pp. 75—77. Nilsson holds that the people of the Bronze Age in Scandinavia were Phœnicians.

[2] Aristotle, quoted by Kenrick, p. 225.

Israelites derived all their vessels and utensils of
bronze; iron they had apparently in their own
land;[1] but the tin which was absolutely needful
if the copper, which they dug out of the hills, was
to be of any use to them, could only reach them
from the few and distant places where it was
found,[2] by the agency of Phœnician merchants.[3]
In inscriptions of the eighteenth and nineteenth
dynasties in Egypt, Phœnician vases of bronze
are frequently mentioned, and figured in the
wall-paintings.[4] Glass-making and pottery were
arts in which the natives of Sidon excelled; and
articles of jewellery and carved ivory, found in
the recent excavation, show the skill and taste
to which they had attained.   It is probable that
the ornaments of the Jewish women, of which we
have so long a catalogue in Isaiah (iii. 18—23),
were almost all of Phœnician workmanship.[5]

---

[1] Deut. viii. 9, " whose stones are iron."
Kenrick, p. 212*ff.*

[2] M. Lénormant (ii., pp. 157, 158) has some very good
remarks, chiefly taken from M. de Rougemont's *L'Age
du Bronze, ou les Sémites en Occident,* on the early importance of the tin-trade; but it would take us too far
from our immediate subject to follow him.

[4] Lénormant, ii., p. 215.

[5] Cp. Heeren, " Historische Werke," xi. 94, note †; and
Nilsson, " Das Bronzealter,—Nachtrag," p. 32.

But when we have given due weight to all these various imports, there will probably be a balance of trade against the Phœnicians, to be adjusted by payments in silver; and this supposition is confirmed by the fact that we can trace a marked depreciation in the comparative value of silver during the Jewish history.[1]

One very important branch of the trade of Phœnicia with Israel remains to be spoken of, that is, the trade in slaves. The Phœnicians were known as slave-dealers from the earliest times. Reference has been made already to the passages in which Homer speaks of their kidnapping young princes and princesses, to sell them across the seas. The chorus in the Helena of Euripides is composed of maidens who had been brought to the Egyptian market by Phœnician merchants. Numberless other instances could be quoted to the same effect;[2] it will be sufficient to notice the fact (which rests upon the authority of Strabo) that at Delos, their principal centre for the western trade, 10,000 slaves had been known to be sold in a single day. We cannot doubt that a large proportion of the

---

[1] I Kings x. 21, 27 ; but cp. Movers, ii., 3, p. 39.
[2] Cp. Movers, ii., 3, pp. 70—86.

slaves that they brought with them from Tyre
or Sidon were drawn from the land of Israel.
It is true that our earliest Greek authorities do
not make· any distinct mention of Hebrew
slaves ; but it is highly probable that they
ranked them under the wider name of Syrians,
which occurs in this connection very frequently.
In the earliest times this commerce seems to
have been the most extensive; under the Judges,
several of the northern tribes, as we have seen
above, were at least partially in subjection to the
Phœnicians,[1] and others were rendered incapable
of resistance by the oppression of the Philistines.
At the same time, in the impoverished and unsettled condition of the Hebrew nation, the ties
of commerce would not be so binding as they
afterwards became.   It was probably in the
reign of David or of Solomon that the treaty
was made, to which we have afterwards references, to the effect that the Phœnicians should
not carry Hebrew slaves out of the country
against their will.[2]   But after the disruption of
Solomon's empire, we find bitter complaints
uttered by the prophets against the Tyrians

---

[1] See Movers, ii., 1, pp. 306 *ff*, and above, p. 52.
[2] Movers, ii., 1, p. 313.

because they had "forgotten the covenant of
brethren," [1] and kidnapped the sons of Judah
and the sons of Jerusalem to sell them to the
Grecians. And when the final overthrow came,
we can fancy the Phœnician merchants flocking
to the camp of the Assyrian or Chaldean army,
just as we find them following in the train of
Alexander even as far as India,[2] and buying,
in the forcible language of Joel, "a boy for the
hire of a harlot, and a girl for a draught of wine."
Doubtless there were many razzias made into
Galilee, during the early and unsettled times,
with the express view of carrying off slaves; the
Canaanites who dwelt in the land might often
be willing, when they had the upper hand, as
was not seldom the case, to sell the subjected
Israelites to their kinsmen on the coast; and
further than this, we find traces of the custom
that a man sold not only his children, but even
himself into slavery.[3] But on the whole it seems
that we must confine this trade to the time of
the decline of the Jewish kingdoms, and to the

---

[1] Amos i. 9; Joel iii. 6.

[2] Arrian, Anab. vi., 22. So also a thousand slave-
dealers followed the Syrian General Nicanor in his campaign against Judas Maccabæus, 1 Macc. iii. 41.

[3] Exod. xxi. 7; Lev. xxv. 39.

period which preceded the establishment of the monarchy.

On the other hand, it was just during the reigns of prosperous princes, and especially that of Solomon, that the Phœnicians had the most powerful and beneficial influence in extending the commerce of the Israelites. The empire of Solomon, as has been noticed already, commanded all the main caravan roads that led into Phœnicia, and a mutual understanding between the two nations was thereby rendered necessary. This seems to have taken the form of mutual concession. At least we find that the Phœnicians, though long in exclusive possession of the extremely profitable trade with Arabia, and so with India,[1] did not make any attempt to check the formidable rivalry of the newly-established ports of Ezion-geber and Elath ; but that Hiram sent thither, for the use of Solomon, " ships, and servants that had knowledge of the sea ; and they went with the servants of Solomon to Ophir,[2] and took thence

[1] Movers, ii., 1, p. 332.

[2] The best authorities (Lassen, Ritter, Ewald, etc.) place Ophir in India ; others hold it to have been Arabia, and to this opinion Mr. Twistleton in the Dictionary of the Bible inclines. The question is of little

four hundred and fifty talents of gold, and brought them to king Solomon."[1] Here we have an instance of friendly co-operation which might have been thought *à priori* exceedingly improbable. On the other hand, the Jews do not seem to have made any attempt to enter into rivalry with the Phœnicians with respect to their Mediterranean trade. Joppa might perhaps have been made available as a harbour sufficiently good for the purpose, though it is at best but a dangerous one. But the numerous stories which we have of the extreme jealousy with which the Phœnicians kept to themselves the knowledge of the navigation of the western seas,[2] incline us very little to believe that they would have allowed any other nation, however closely allied to them, to share their profitable secrets. The case of the Arabian trade was different, because they had never had intercourse with these fertile regions except by land; and they would have lost much more by the interruption of this traffic

importance to the present discussion. Cp. Ewald, iii., p. 77 ; Max Müller, Lectures, i., p. 202*ff.*

[1] 2 Chron. viii. 18, cp. ix. 10, and 1 Kings ix. 27.

[2] See Kenrick, p. 190. Blakesley's Herodotus, Introduction.

than they could have lost by the rivalry of any sea-traders, especially when they seem themselves to have enjoyed equal privileges with the latter. It is generally admitted now that "the navy of Tarshish" spoken of in the Biblical narrative only denotes large ships, such as those that used to be sent to Tarshish, and does not by any means imply any direct commerce on the part of Solomon with Tartessus.[1] That this navy did not go to Spain is evident from the mention of ivory, apes, and peacocks among the things that were brought back in it.[2]

If we now come to consider what was the effect of this constant and extensive commerce between Phœnicia and Israel, we shall find it very various and far-reaching. There is of course, in the first place, the purely economic effect. The one great benefit arising from international commerce is that each nation is hereby enabled to employ its productive forces more

---

[1] Cp. Ewald, iii., p. 76, note 1 ; Kenrick, p. 357. This supposition however implies an error on the part of the writer of 2 Chron. ix. 21. Cp. (or contrast) E. H. P. in Dict. Bible, iii., p. 1347*b*, and E. T., *ib.*, 1440*a*.

[2] With all Ewald's dogmatism, it is hardly fair for Mr. Plumptre to pass this objection of his over without discussion as "arbitrary."

efficiently,—that is to say, each produces a larger amount of wealth than it would otherwise have produced, because each nation is able to devote its energies wholly to that which it can do best, leaving any needs that this does not satisfy to be met by supplies from without.[1] The nation of Israel was much the wealthier, because it was able to give itself almost entirely to agriculture and the simpler form of manufacture, leaving the finer manufactures and the products of more elaborate art to be furnished by Phœnicia. And wealth so acquired brings with it a certain increase in civilization. Tastes are developed, ideas enlarged, and graceful forms and beautiful colours brought into homes which would otherwise have remained in ignorant simplicity. But advantages of this kind may easily be bought too dear. The first and plainest result was perhaps the most conspicuous in the northern kingdom. The gulf between the rich and the poor became widened ; the former in the luxury and wantonness of their life gave way to drunkenness and licentiousness of every kind, and the latter were oppressed

[1] That this is the true view is clearly shown by Mr. Mill, Political Economy, book iii., c. xvii., § 3.

and down-trodden miserably. The prophets
who were sent to the land of Israel shortly
before the fall of Samaria, give us a terrible
picture of the moral degradation of the people.
" They have erred through wine, and through
strong drink are gone out of the way; the
priest and the prophet have erred through strong
drink, they are swallowed up with wine, they
are out of the way through strong drink; they
err in vision, they stumble in giving judgment:
for all places are full of vomit and filthiness, so
that there is no place clean."[1] Even great ladies,
who are compared to the fat cows or heifers
of Bashan, that fed on the rich mountains of
Samaria, say to their lords, " Bring and let us
drink."[2] The Lord had a controversy with the
inhabitants of the land, because there was
neither truth nor mercy nor knowledge of God;
only by swearing and lying and killing and
stealing and committing adultery, one vast inun-
dation of crime was sweeping over the country.[3]
Of course all this was not the result solely of the
influx of wealth. But it is not too much to say
that it was mainly, if not entirely, due to the

[1] Is. xxviii. 7, 8.   [3] Hosea, iv. 1, 2 (Pusey).
[2] Stanley, ii., p. 359.

Phœnician influence, and that this influence was immensely strengthened by the material advantages of a close connection with the cities of the coast. The house of Omri had greatly promoted the influx of the foreign civilization by the marriage of Ahab with Jezebel, daughter of Ethbaal, and had extended it to the southern kingdom by the alliance of Athaliah with Jehoram, the son of Jehoshaphat. And Athaliah, "matre turpi filia turpior," guided her son Ahaziah in the ways of the house of Ahab, for his mother was his counsellor to do wickedly.[1] But however great the effect of these unholy alliances may have been for the time, we cannot doubt that the main cause of the evil lay much deeper and was far more permanent. It was not the example of one or two powerful and wicked queens that could taint the fountain of the nation's life. There was a large leaven of the old Canaanite element left in the land by the cowardice, sloth, and disobedience of the earliest conquerors, which must have been constantly exercising a corrupting influence. But the most pernicious action was probably that of the traders brought into the land by the commerce

[1] 2 Chron. xxii. 4.

with Phœnicia. Many of these were only travelling merchants, but their repeated visits would
not be without effect. In the first place, we
have reason to believe that their commercial
morality was low ; " Phœnician lies" were proverbial,[1] and wherever violence was out of the
question (as must have been usually the case
in their dealings with the Israelites) they would
have recourse to any mean and dishonest trickery
to secure the enormous profits which their
trade seems generally to have brought them.[2]
Perhaps the originators, certainly the most in-
fluential disseminators, of that system of weights
and measures which, under the name of "Babylonian" (as Böckh[3] has shown) was widely current in the East, it may well be supposed that
they would often take advantage of the ignorance and simplicity of the rustic population to
defraud them for their own advantage. We
have seen in our own time, and unhappily sometimes with our own countrymen, too many
instances of the evil wrought by unfair dealing

[1] See quotations in Kenrick, p. 190, and Movers, ii., 3,
p. 105.

[2] Cp. Hosea xii. 8 : " As for the Canaanite, deceitful
balances are in his hand."

[3] " Metrologische Untersuchungen," Abschn. viii.

with native tribes, at first unsuspecting, and then all-suspecting, to fail to recognize the mischief that must have been done in this way by the Phœnician merchants to their Palestinian neighbours.

But this was not all. The wares in which they dealt were often not less pernicious than their method of dealing. The character of a nation's art cannot fail to be deeply affected by the nature of its religion; and when we come to see what the religion of the Phœnicians was, we shall be able to understand that the numerous objects of art that they were constantly bringing .into Israel may have tended greatly to corrupt it. There are chambers in the Museo Borbonico which show us that what has now to be hidden away from the eyes of men, was even in the Italian cities freely presented in the ornaments and even the utensils of ordinary life. What was possible in Pompeii and Herculaneum is hardly likely to have been wanting in the factories of Tyre and Sidon. The famous Sidonian πέπλοι, necklaces, earrings, and bracelets, may have been, and probably were, all wrought so as to do honour to the deities of Phœnicia, and grievous dishonour to the Holy

9

One of Israel, who is of purer eyes than to look upon iniquity.[1]

But besides these travelling "Canaanites," there were other merchants who were settlers in the land for a longer time, and whose influence would be the more powerful, as it was so continuous.[2] In the later times they seem to have been confined to a suburb "before the gate" of the town, which they chose for their habitation, but there are many traces in the earlier literature of their residence in the midst of the burghers.[3] The luxury and at the same time the shameless profligacy of these wealthy resident merchants are strikingly depicted in the account of the strange [*i.e.* foreign] woman in the Book of Proverbs, "which flattereth with her words."[4] Her husband is evidently a trader who has gone his rounds to make purchases in the country districts, which he will bring back to the city by the day appointed, *i.e.* (according to the mar-

---

[1] Cp. Movers, i., p. 52.

[2] Movers has collected many passages relating to this class of traders in vol. ii., part 3, pp. 112—126. Cp. i., p. 49 *ff.*

[3] Cp. Neh. xiii. 16, 20, and Zeph. i. 10, 11, with Zach. xiv. 21, Joel iv. 17 ; and see Movers, ii., 3, p. 202.

[4] Cp. the use of *peregrina* in Donat. ad Ter. Eunuch., i., 2, 27 ; and see Movers, i., p. 53.

ginal rendering and De Wette) in time for the
fair at the appearance of the new moon.[1] Well
might the wise king utter his words of warning
against this foreign temptress, "for she hath
cast down many wounded; yea, many strong
men have been slain by her. Her house is the
way to the grave, going down to the chambers
of death." That these alluring but accursed
portals were open in every city, was due in no
small measure to the influence of the Phœnician
commerce.

But where the Tyrian and Sidonian merchants were gathered, as often, in large communities, other and still more dangerous influences
were brought to work. For we find it a constant
article of stipulation in the commercial treaties
that have been preserved to us, that the settlers
should live in the free exercise of their national
customs and religion. This involved the erection of shrines to Baal and Moloch, the dedi-
cation of groves to Astarte, and therewith the
constant presence of a fascinating kind of
temptation, before the eyes of a people already
disposed to fall before it. The "high places
which were before Jerusalem, which were on the

On these fairs see Movers, ii., 3, pp. 135*ff*, 146.

right hand of the mount of corruption, which Solomon the king of Israel had builded for Ashtoreth the abomination of the Sidonians,"[1] may have had their origin in the idolatrous wishes of one of his wives ; but they were certainly maintained during the centuries which elapsed before they were destroyed by Josiah, by the Tyrian merchants who dwelt in the quarter of Jerusalem known as Machtesh.[2] It is probable indeed that Josiah was emboldened to take this step by the fact that his hostility to Egypt necessarily involved a breach of all friendly relations with Phœnicia.[3] The subsequent section of this essay will furnish a more fit occasion for discussing the influence of this worship at length. It will be sufficient here to notice that this was probably the greatest of all the curses that Phœnician intercourse brought upon the Jews, sapping their national life at its very basement, and by inevitable laws bringing upon them the degradation, the ruin, and the shame that must visit every nation, in these days

---

[1] 2 Kings xxiii. 13.

[2] Cp. Zeph. i. 11 (with Henderson's note), and Movers, i., p. 50.

[3] See above, p. 84.

as in days of old, where vice is identified with pleasure, and woman has grown impure.

Mr. Gladstone has probably gone much too far in assigning almost all that is evil in the religion of Greece to Phœnician influence.[1] If it would not lead too far from the present subject, it would be easy to show, on the one hand, that many of the myths which he regards as Phœnician are the common property of the Aryan race, and, on the other hand, that pure and beautiful as they were at the beginning, they were yet capable of a natural, and all but inevitable misinterpretation, which should change their fresh young grace into loathsome foulness. But whatever may have been the case with the Greeks, it cannot be doubted that to the Hebrew nation the Phœnicians played the part of the serpent in the Mosaic account of primitive man. They gave to the simple tribes, preserved, if not in innocence, at least in comparative purity, by the hardy life of the desert, the fruit of the tree of the knowledge of good and evil, and they did eat. And the eyes at least of the noblest among them, the " Seers,"

[1] *Quarterly Review*, January, 1868, and Juventus Mundi, *passim.*

were opened, and they were ashamed, and the burning language which gushed forth from them[1] remains to us still as the most impressive warning to those who for love of luxury, of sloth, or of lust forsake their fathers' God, and turn to the idols that are worshipped by those who seem to be prospering round about them.

But there is another and a brighter side to this page in the history of the Chosen People, which it were faithless not to recognize. As the Fall was, in Schiller's daring words, a gigantic stride in the development of humanity, so that which is in some respects its antitype in Hebrew history can be and ought to be regarded in the same light. Those whose joy it is to trace, so far as they may, the methods of the Divine education of the world, will not fail to notice how, after the centuries of national vice and ever-increasing degradation had borne their bitter fruit in the desolation of the national life, the Jewish people came forth from the trial weakened, scattered, and all but crushed, but

[1] The literal meaning of the Hebrew word for " prophet" seems to be " one who involuntarily bursts forth with spiritual utterances." See Gesenius in voc. *Nabi*, and Stanley, vol. i., lect. xix.

henceforth never to be shaken in their fidelity to the One Living God, and never as a nation to relapse into the sensual vice inseparable from Eastern idolatry.[1] We may venture to believe that the struggle of the Church with the moral corruption of pagan Greece and Rome was greatly aided by the fact that it found in every city a leaven of faithful Jewish preachers of chastity and self-control. And this the Jews could never have become, had they not been suffered to drink to the bitter dregs the Circe cup of the great Phœnician enchantress, by whose sorceries the nations were deceived.

[1] "The results of this discipline of the Jewish nation may be summed up in two points—a settled national belief in the unity and spirituality of God, and an acknowledgment of the paramount importance of chastity as a point of morals."—The Bishop of Exeter, in "Essays and Reviews," p. 11. It is perhaps worth while adding, that the passage in the text, and a similar one at the close of the following chapter, were written eight or nine years after I had read Dr. Temple's essay, when all conscious recollection of his argument had been lost ; and that it was only on reading the essay again that I found how completely his view coincided with that to which an entirely different course of discussion had appeared to lead.

CHAPTER II.

THE RELIGION OF PHŒNICIA, AND ITS INFLUENCE UPON ISRAEL.

Early Monotheism, Aryan and Semitic—Traces of Polytheism— Israel in Egypt—Tendency to Idolatry there—Their Religious Condition in the Desert—The Religion of Canaan and Phœnicia—Baal worshipped under various aspects—Worship of Ashtoreth—El worshipped by all Semitic Nations—History of Baal-worship in Israel—Conclusion.

THE recent researches of comparative mythologists carry us back to a period in the history of the Aryan races of which it may be said that polytheism was not yet in existence. The purely philological arguments of M. Pictet,[1] deeply interesting as they are, would not of themselves perhaps carry conviction with them. But more value may be attached to the conclusions which are drawn from a study of the oldest remains of literature. Homer has more

[1] Les Aryas Primitifs, vol. ii., pp. 652—660, and pp. 707—728.

than one passage in which the light of a purer
faith is seen struggling through the clouds and
darkness of a comparatively late mythology.
And the Vedas speak in yet clearer language.
We find there, it is true, the names of several
gods'; by the side of the supreme Dyaus are
Indra, and Varuna, Sûrya and Vishnu, to say
nothing of more evident personifications, like
Agni and the Maruts. But Professor Max
Müller has taught us to see in these no distinct
abandonment of the faith in the One Supreme.
Rather, the worshipper in every case addresses
himself to that embodiment of the Divine and
Invisible Spirit to which his thoughts at the
time were most immediately directed. Sometimes he regards Him as the all-embracing
heaven, "hoc sublimen candens, quem omnes
inuocant Iouem;"[1] sometimes as the life-giving
sun ; sometimes again as the Lord of Thunder,
that dashes apart with his bolt the stormy
clouds, and makes them yield to men the trea-
sures of rain that they bear within them. But
in all cases it seems to be the One Great God
to whom he is offering his prayers and praises,
putting out of his mind entirely for the time the

---

[1] Ennius in Cic. de Nat. Deor., ii., § 4.

other forms in which the Deity is supposed to manifest Himself to mortals. It is easy to see how this poetic language would become in time the natural parent of a numerous and finally a debasing progeny of legends. But the great gift which comparative mythology, the youngest of the sciences, has given to us, is the increased conviction that it was not with the vile and shameful, but rather with the pure and simple, if as yet all vague and childlike thoughts of the Divine, that the souls of our earliest progenitors were filled. Unfortunately, we have not hitherto succeeded in obtaining anything like the same amount of evidence with regard to the early beliefs of the Semitic peoples. But all the indications that we are able to find seem to be converging towards a period of a somewhat similar creed. M. Rénan delights to dwell upon the " natural instinct " of the Semitic peoples towards monotheism ;[1] but the facts of the case bear out his theory only to a very limited extent. It is true that the branch of the Semites which he calls the Térachites (the

[1] In his " Histoire des Langues Semitiques," and in a. separate brochure, " Nouvelles Considerations sur le Caractère général des peuples Semitiques, et en particulier sur leur Tendance au Monothéisme."

sons of Terah), has remained for the most part faithful to its belief in the One God ; but with the second, the " political " branch, the reverse is notoriously the case. Professor Max Müller has attacked M. Rénan's theory of a " monotheistic instinct," with all his wonted ability,[1] and traces the comparative absence of polytheism among the Semites to their freedom from the allurements of mythological language ; but the firm adhesion to the unity of the Deity to a special revelation made to Abraham. Be this as it may, we find in the earliest times among the Semites just the same tendency, as among the Aryans, to regard the Divine Spirit as embodying Himself under various forms for the worship of individual nations. This was probably not so much the recognition of different gods, as the acknowledgment that different nations might worship the same great Power under various names and aspects. But by degrees, at least with the Hebrews, the conception was somewhat modified ; and they seem to have come to the belief that there were many gods, each with his own nation, to watch over and support to the best of his power, but

[1] Chips, etc., i., pp. 342—380.

that their own God, Jehovah, or rather Jahveh,
was by far the greatest of all in power and
purity. We know, for instance, that Terah and
his family served " other gods " than the God of
Abraham,[1] and that in the days of Joshua it
might be at least regarded as an open question
whether the nation should serve these deities of
their early ancestors, or the gods of the Amorites, in whose land they dwelt, or Jahveh, the
God of the Mosaic law. And though the nation, animated and impressed by the noble
words of Joshua, renewed their covenant with
Jahveh, "who had brought them out of Egypt,"
still we can see that this was not regarded as
the only possible alternative. There was danger
not only of forsaking Jahveh, but also of serving
other gods, the gods of the nations round them.
Monotheism, in the strictest sense of the term,
can scarcely be regarded as the "instinct " of a
people to whom the challenge of Joshua was
possible. Traces of the same feeling are to be
found late in the subsequent literature of the
nation. For instance: "Among the gods, there
is none like unto Thee, O Jahveh ; neither are
there any works like unto Thy works." Nor could

[1] Joshua xxiv. 2.

a poet have spoken of God as "the great king above all gods," had the gods of the heathen been recognized by him as what they really were—"mighty shadows thrown by the mighty works of God, and intercepting for a time the pure light of the Godhead."[1]

Plainer traces of polytheism are to be found in the teraphim of Laban and of Rachel, which are enough of themselves to show that the lofty spiritual views of the head of the family could not always be communicated to other and especially to female members of it.

The readiness even of a man like Abraham to recognize other conceptions of the Divine than that which he had formed for himself, comes out clearly in the story, undoubtedly extremely ancient,[2] of his intercourse with Melchisedec. At the time the Father of the Faithful worshipped El Shaddai, the Omnipotent, and had not yet been permitted to know the full meaning of the name Jahveh, even if the word was

---

[1] Max Müller, Chips, i., p. 371. We must not lose sight of passages like "All the gods of the nations are idols," but they are found almost exclusively in the writings of the later psalmists. Cp. Ewald, ii., pp. 122, 123.

[2] Ewald, i., p. 321.

already used by him.[1] The Canaanite Priest-
King, retaining the simplicity of what we have
reason to believe was the earliest faith, but
clothing his creed in different language, worshipped El Eliun,[a] the highest God, possessor
of heaven and earth. We cannot fail to be re-
minded here of the passage of Sanchoniathon,
which tells us of Eliun, called Hypsistus (ὕψιστος)
of whom was begotten Epigeus, whom they
afterwards called Ouranos, and who had a sister
by the same parents, called Ge. In all the confusion of this genealogical cosmogony, we seem
to trace the remembrance of an old Semitic conception, vivid and true in the days of Mel-
chisedek, but obscured by the bewildering aftergrowth of Phœnician mythology. At any rate
Abraham did not fail to acknowledge the unity
that lay beneath the apparent diversity, and in
his oath by "Jahveh, the most high God, the
possessor [or Creator] of heaven and earth," he
identifies the two conceptions. Both these tendencies,—the one leading to the recognition of

---

[1] Cp. Exod. vi. 3. The Bishop of Natal ("The Pentateuch," part v., chap. xix.) endeavours to prove the
Phœnician origin of the name Jahveh ; I think with little
success. Movers decidedly opposes this theory.

Gen, xiv. 18—22. Cp. De Wette's version.

gods other than the national Jehovah, and greatly, immeasurably inferior to Him, and the other that which saw under various names the same great Deity ; the latter the more philosophically true, the former perhaps the better preservative against temptations from without, —will be found of vast importance in the subsequent religious history of Israel.

The sojourn in Egypt was undoubtedly a crisis of as much importance for the religious as for the national life of the Hebrew people. On the one hand, many of their number seem to have fallen into positive idolatry. "Put away the gods," says Joshua,[1] "which your fathers served on the other side of the flood [*i.e.* the river Euphrates], and in Egypt." Ezekiel[2] brings the charge as plainly: "Then said I unto them, cast ye away every man the abominations of his eyes, and defile not yourselves with the idols of Egypt ; I Jahveh am your God. But they rebelled against me, and would not hearken unto me : they did not every man cast away the abominations of their eyes, neither did they forsake the idols of Egypt." But it is curious to notice that in the specific charges brought

xxiv. 14.   [2] xx. 7, 8. Cp. also xxiii. 3.

against the people by Amos (v. 26), and repeated by St. Stephen (Acts vii. 43), it is not
distinctly Egyptian deities that they are said to
have worshipped. They "took up 'the tabernacle of Moloch, and the star of their god
Remphan (or according to Amos Chiun[1]), figures
which they made to worship them." Now to
say nothing of Moloch, who certainly was not
Egyptian, the best authorities (*e. g.* Mr. R. S.
Poole, in the Dictionary of the Bible, *s. v.*
Remphan) teach us that Remphan and Chiun
[Renpu and Ken] were in Egypt foreign deities,
probably Phœnician, and identical with Baal
and Astarte. They were worshipped in Lower
Egypt, and Mr. Poole thinks that the presence
of a large foreign population there points to the
fact that the shepherd-kings were still in power
at the time of the Exodus. But apart from the
probability that the Israelites adopted this idolatrous worship during the earlier years of their
sojourn in the land, there is little ground for
supposing that all the Canaanitish population
should have been expelled with the Hyksos
dynasty. It is much more probable that a
large body remained in Egypt, to be subjected

But see LXX. version of Amos.

to the same oppression as the children of Israel,[1]
and possibly to join them in their final Exodus.

On the other hand, if we find already proofs
of the attraction of the Phœnician idolatry, we
know also that this was the time of the con-
solidation of that pure religion that was destined to struggle against it for so many centuries,
and, often defeated for the time, to win the victory at last for all succeeding ages, " saved so as
by fire." Here was developed first the idea of
the *Theocracy*—" one among many kinds of rule
and polity ; as unstable and changeable as any
other ; passing through the most varied changes
and admixtures in Israel, often distorted until
all likeness was lost, and weakened so as to
threaten total decay ; and in semblance found
among other nations of antiquity ; and yet, in
its actual form, unique in this one people, and
wholly new on earth—the sole true life and un-
dying breath of its history, always renewing
itself on the deepest basis, all chances and
changes notwithstanding, and in the course of
its development only unfolding itself again to a
fuller and riper perfection, till at length it attains
to the only true and adequate realization possible

[1] Exod. xii. 38 : Numbers xi. 4; cp. Ewald, ii., p. 82.

to it,"[1] in the spiritual rule of the King that rules
in righteousness, mighty to save.

The religion of the Egyptians was too sensuous, too subtle, and too formal and petty in
its details to present any very great attractions
to the simpler and less artificial Hebrews; and
it was soon made still more distasteful to them
when its adherents became their cruel oppressors. So, led by the genius and the inspiration
of Moses, they embraced with eagerness the
great conception of a National God, Jahveh the
Deliverer, before whom the gods of the heathen
were not Elohim, but Elilim; not gods, but
rather no-gods.[2] We cannot ascribe to Moses
anything like a complete revelation of the character of the Deity. The literature of the nation
as late as some, not only of the Davidic, but of
the later Psalms,[3] shows us how imperfect was
the knowledge even then of "the Lord God,
merciful and gracious, pardoning iniquity and
transgression," and requiring His people to follow the Divine Example. But to Moses we
may fairly assign, in the words of Ewald,[4] "the
"pure healthy germ of all truth respecting a

---

[1] Ewald, ii., p. 1.   [3] Psalms xxxv., lxix., etc.
[2] Ewald, ii., p. 123.   [4] ii., p. 54.

spiritual God, and the first powerful inexhaustible impulse given by the establishment of the community to the enduring preservation and fruitful development of that germ." Novalis has called Spinoza a " Gott trunkner Mann." The epithet is dubious in this application of it; it would have been more just if applied to Spinoza's nation. When once they had risen to the conception of a Divine Being, who had taken them to Him as a people, and was unto them a God; when once they had found the true Deliverer,[1] for whom the pagan nations were blindly feeling, if haply they might find Him (though He was not far from any one of them) ; when they knew Him to be their special Healer (Ex. xv. 26) and Guide into the Land of Promise,[2] they won a sense of His living presence, and continuous activity amongst them, to which nothing in the ancient world is comparable.

This intimate relation with the Unseen and the Divine did not confine itself to the sphere of the spiritual. A Psalm like the hundred and fourth, or a passage like Job xxxvi.—xxxviii., is enough

---

[1] Cp. Ewald, ii., p. 109*ff.*

[2] Cp. the beautiful ἐτροφοφόρησεν of Acts xiii. 18. (Lachmann and Tischendorf.)

to show how in every operation of nature they
delighted to see the working of the Holy One
of Israel. But it was the sense of the possible
communion of spirit with spirit, a communion
utterly foreign to the pagan mind, that gave
its strength to the religion of Moses. To quote
once more from the great historian whose piety,
profundity, and eloquence make us regret the
more deeply his arbitrary dogmatism: "He
whose spirit finds its true place in the Eternal
Spirit, in that act receives an infinite power,
which raises him above the world and time, and
suffers him to find rest only where the most
blessed contentment dwells in union with an
unfailing zeal to participate in the Divine
energy. . . . With the fundamental thought of
God the Deliverer, there arise within the human
soul at once the ability and the courage to
recognize all the truth of the Divine Spirit who
confronts it, and to open itself to his living influence. And this is a life which, when once it
has struck vigorous root among men, can never
perish, but advances with ever-multiplying fruits.
. . . Here then we perceive in its germ that
which made the history of the ancient people of
Israel a world-history ; that while among other

nations that torpidity of soul, paganism, was assuming more and more rigid forms, until it became quite incurable by the few scattered spirits among them who looked deeper, and attempted bolder things, among the Israelites, even in a relatively very early time, and before the heathenish tendencies in them could be fully unfolded, that freedom and boldness of spirit grew up, which, after once beholding the purity and power of the Divine light, can never wholly weary of turning towards it a larger and fuller gaze."[1] The heathenish tendencies again and again broke out during the desert wanderings ; even at the foot of Sinai, the timorous people made for themselves a golden calf, possibly as a symbol of Jahveh's presence, but possibly also in honour of the "heifer-Baal"[2] that they had learnt to worship in Lower Egypt;—the licentious dances which accompanied the worship confirm this latter view. The lonely desert life kept them free from the temptations of foreign idolatry, and the only instance of any attempt to forsake the service of Jahveh was when one of the

[1] Ewald, ii., p. 112.

[2] Tobit, i., 5, cp. Dict. Bible, iii., 1028*b*. But see on the other hand Ewald, ii., p. 183 ; his treatment of the whole incident seems to be in his most arbitrary style.

"mixed multitude" blasphemed the *Name*. The punishment appointed by the law followed at once, the offender was stoned, and we hear no more of any unfaithfulness. We do not wonder to find the prophet Hosea long years afterwards speaking of the desert as the place where communion with God was the closest (ii. 14—20): "Behold, I will guide her tenderly, and bring her into the wilderness, and speak unto her heart;[1] and from thence I will give her vineyards, and the valley of trouble for a door of hope, and she shall sing[2] there as in the days of her youth, and as in the day when she came up out of the land of Egypt. . . . For I will take away the names of Baalim out of her mouth, and they shall be no more remembered by their name. And I will betroth thee unto me for ever; yea, I will betroth thee unto me in righteousness, and in judgment, and in lovingkindness, and in mercies: I will even betroth thee unto me in faithfulness; and thou shalt know the Lord." One omen of evil alone clouded the brightness of their glad and triumphant entrance into the Land of Promise. Balak, the king of Moab, had sum-

Cp. the Hebrew.

[2] "Intellege autem carmen fletûset precum."—*Gesenius.*

moned Balaam to curse the goodly tents of
Jacob; the prophetic utterances had only taken
the form of blessing, but the treacherous coun-
sels of the seer were far more fatal than any
imprecation. It was not improbably at his suggestion that the Midianites " called the people
unto the sacrifices of their gods ; and the people
did eat, and bowed down to their gods ; and
Israel joined himself to Baal-Peor ; and the
anger of the Lord was kindled against Israel."
The character of the worship is plainly shown
by the derivation of the name of the god, his
identification by Jerome with Priapus,[1] and the
story of Zimri and Cozbi. But we must not fail
to notice that if there were some of the children
of Israel ready to fall before shameful temptation, the worship was by no means general, and
was suppressed with terrible severity by the indignation of Moses, supported by the elders and
the majority of the community. We must consider this episode as a proof rather of the weak-
ness of a portion of the nation, than of a wide-
spread corruption and apostasy. On the whole,
it was a nation of loyal and faithful worshippers
of Jahveh, strong with a vivid consciousness of

[1] Cp. Hosea ix. 10.

His favour and His power to bless, that crossed
the Jordan under the command of Joshua.

We have now to endeavour to gain a clear
conception of the religion of the tribes with
whom the struggle had to be waged, and of the
wealthy and powerful maritime cities with which
the invaders would be brought into close and
constant intercourse.

Here we have still less difficulty than we had
before in deciding upon the substantial identity
of Phœnicians and Canaanites. Even those
scholars who contend for an original distinction
of race, would not deny that at the time of the
invasion of the children of Israel the deities
worshipped on the coast and in the inland cities
were substantially the same. Substantially, and
not exactly; for there are several lesser divi-
nities of the Sidonians which do not appear to
have been known or worshipped by the Canaanites. But the basis of their religious beliefs,
and no small part of the superstructure, were
precisely identical.

Phœnician polytheism—we might almost say
all polytheism—had its origin in nature-worship.
By this I do not mean fetish-worship, which the
Positive philosophy, with its usual arbitrary dog-

matism, asserts to have been the earliest stage
in all human development. Of such a stage we
do not find a trace. Much rather, one section
of the early Semites, probably that which we
have already referred to as having been the first
to leave the original home in the mountains of
Kurdistan, went through an experience analogous
to that of some divisions of the Aryan stock.
For these, at least, M. Rénan's words are of
dubious accuracy: "Ayant détaché beaucoup
plus tôt sa personnalité de l'univers, elle en
conclut presque immédiatement le troisième
terme, Dieu créateur de l'univers ; au lieu d'une
nature animée et vivante dans toutes ses parties,
elle conçut, si j'ose le dire, une nature séche et
sans fécondité."[1] On the contrary, the Canaanite
peoples, looking out into the world around them,

---

[1] Histoire, etc., p. 497. His words form a striking contrast with those of M. Lenormant. "The divine being,
the primordial Baal, was almost identified with the
material world. He was superlatively a nature-god, ope-
rating in the universe, and in physical life, each year de-
stroying his work, to renew it afresh with the change of
seasons ; and these successive operations of destruction
and renewal, in consequence of the pantheistic conception
of his essence, he was regarded as producing, not in a
world created by him, but in his own proper person, by a
reaction on himself." (ii. 220.)

ınusing on the ceaseless marvel of birth and life
and death, and deeply influenced, we may well
believe, by the Cushite empire of Chaldæa,[1] near
which their earliest settlements had been,
thought that they saw at work beneath the phenomena of nature two great principles, one the
creative, the other the receptive. To these cor-
responded the phenomena of the earliest and
deepest mystery of human life, summed up in
the words, " So God created man ; male and
female created He them." So each of these
principles was embodied in a personal conception ; the life-giving force of nature was worshipped under the name of Baal, "the Lord ;"[2]
Chemosh, "the governor ;" Hadad, "the only
one ;" Moloch, "the king ;" or sometimes simply
El, "the God." The purely receptive faculty
was adored as Ashtoreth, as Baalith, or as Atar-
gath. But these conceptions did not remain as
purely ideal. Movers has well defined the
Phœnician religion as " an apotheosis of the
forces and laws of nature ; *an adoration of the
objects in which those forces were seen, and where*

---

[1] Especially with regard to the *astral* character of their
religion. Cp. Movers, i., p. 80, and see below.

[2] Perhaps more properly "owner," cp. Movers, i., p. 171.
See Lenormant, ii., p. 219.

they appeared most active." Hence it came about that Baal was not only the vivifying principle, but also the lord of its concrete embodiment, the life-giving sun : he wâs the god of fire, " sic enim se res habet," as Cicero (de Nat. Deor. II. § 23) puts it, " ut omnia quae aluntur atque crescunt, contineant in se vim caloris, sine qua neque ali possent nec crescere." But as the sun calls into being things evil as well as good, and out of death brings forth corruption, so he was Baal-zebub, " the god of flies," who was able to bring this plague upon those who neglected his worship. Further, as being the highest of all the heavenly ones, he was identified with the planet Saturn, according to the ancient conceptions[1] the most distant and exalted of the Cabirim, " the powerful ones." But under all these manifestations, he was (originally at least) one and the same god,[2] viewed in different aspects, but always regarded for the time as the supreme, and hence identified by the Greeks with Zeus. Side by side with this tendency to distinguish the several functions of Baal, by the creation of individual hypostases each setting forth some

[1] See Tac. Hist., v., 4, quoted below.
[2] Movers, i., p. 172*ff.*

whether intended as a relapse into the worship
of Elohim as distinguished from Jahveh, or
more probably merely a symbolic representation of the national God, seems to have owed
nothing to Phœnician influence, but rather to
have been drawn from Egypt, where Jeroboam
had for a time resided.   But the name of the
city calls our attention to one of the most
ancient and obscure cults of Canaan.   In
Phœnicia, and therefore probably in the surrounding tribes, a common object of worship
was the baetyl or upright stone, such as that
described by Tacitus[1] as found in the temple of
the Paphian Venus : "simulacrum Deae non
effigie humana, continuus orbis latiore initio
tenuem in ambitum, metae modo, exsurgens."
Movers[2] has collected many references to such
pillar-like erections ; and it is hard to resist his
argument that these, like the wooden columns of
the Asherah, had originally a phallic character.
It is probable then that Bethel, as the seat of
this rude and primitive worship,[3] retained a kind

[1] Hist. ii., 3.

[2] i., pp. 673—675, cp. 567—572, 593—597.

[3] The older etymologers, *e.g.*, Spencer, "de Legg.
Hebr.," 444, and Bochart, " Canaan," ii., 2, were inclined
to derive the word βαιτύλιον from " Bethel," as being the

of sacred reputation, which made it the object of the choice of Jeroboam, as one of the religious centres of the northern kingdom. But the prophets of the golden calves still called themselves the prophets of Jahveh,[1] and the national apostasy only began really with the house of Omri. There are several reasons for believing that he it was, rather than his son Ahab, who was the first of the kings of Israel to give his support to the worship of Baal. He appears to have been an active, energetic king, and to have formed alliances with the neighbouring nations, one result of which was the free admission of their subjects into his new capital, for " he made streets " for the Tyrians in Samaria. And he seems to have been responsible for the marriage of his son with the Tyrian Jezebel, which was soon to be so fatal to the national religion. Hence it is that Micah (vi. 16) mentions among the sins of the children of Israel, that " the statutes of Omri were strictly kept, and all the work of the house of Ahab." The political cir-

name of the place where the most famous sacred stone was found ; and Mr. Grove (" Dict. Bible," i., p. 198a) does not reject the derivation. Cp. Mr. W. A. Wright's article on " Idols " (ib., p. 850a).

[1] See Ewald, iii., p. 155.

cumstances of the time, which made a Tyrian alliance attractive, have been already referred to.[1]

But it was mainly to Jezebel that the formal introduction of the worship of Baal was due. The many causes that combined to help this on had hitherto been at least partially counter-acted by the zeal and energy of the prophetic order, who were devoted to the worship of Jahveh. But now these were fiercely perse-cuted ; and the boundless influence of the queen over her weak but sometimes well-meaning hus-band, swept away all open resistance. Only those prophets who were hidden away from her fury escaped ; and her national religion was established in the land of Jahveh. A temple of great magnificence was built in honour of Baal, where four hundred priests served his shrine ; and an oracular grove was erected to Ashtoreth,[2] where besides the four hundred and fifty pro-phets of the grove that fed at Jezebel's table, there were undoubtedly many of the kede-shoth, of whom we read in the later prophets.[3]

[1] See p. 67.

[2] Ewald, iii., p. 172.

[3] Hosea iv. 14 ; cp. Gen. xxxviii. 21, 22, and Deut. xxiii. 17.

The extent to which this worship was adopted by the nation is shown by the fact that there were only seven thousand in Israel, knees which had not bowed to Baal, and lips which had not kissed him.

The display of Divine power on Carmel, contrasted with the wild but futile efforts of the priests of the Tyrian deities to call forth a response from the objects of their worship, aroused for the time an enthusiasm for the God of Israel. But it seems to have exhausted itself in the vengeance taken on the foreign priests, and Elijah felt that there was no strong national feeling upon which he could rely to protect him against the revenge of the furious queen. He fled into the desert, there to lay him down and die. But his work, like all true work for God, was not destined to perish unavailingly, though he might not see the fruit of it. We cannot but believe that the memory of the grand old prophet, of his words of bitter scorn and bold defiance, served as a powerful assistance to Jehu in his work of reformation. He would hardly have ventured, even by an act of treachery, to deal such terrible retribution upon the worshippers of Baal, had he not felt assured of the

support, or at least the indifference, of a great
body of the nation. At the same time the very
fact that at the critical point of his usurpation
he was not afraid to give himself out as a
worshipper of Baal, even with his hostile object,
shows that the indignation against the foreign
deities cannot have been really strong. Dean
Stanley is merely speaking somewhat loosely,
when he says that " a sweeping massacre removed at one blow the whole heathen population of Israel."[1] We cannot suppose that
anything like all those who worshipped Baal,
or even all who were fanatically devoted to his
worship, were to be found at one time within his
courts, even on a solemn occasion. It is much
more probable that from this time there was
a constant internal conflict in the kingdom of
Israel between the two religions. Perhaps we
ought rather to say the three religions; for while
we find a constant succession of prophets uphold-
ing the purity of the worship of Jahveh, and learn
from the writings of such as have remained to
us that many of the people were still devoted to
Baal, the court appears to have held to what
may be called the State religion, the worship of

[1] Dict. Bible, i., p. 961*a.*

the Golden Calf. All three forms are brought
before us in a passage from our great authority
on this period, the prophet Hosea :[1] " When
Ephraim spake there was trembling ; he exalted
himself in Israel ; but he offended in Baal, and
died : and now they go on to sin, and make
for themselves molten images, idols of silver,
according to their skill ; all of them the work
of artificers ; the men that sacrifice say of them,
let them kiss the calves ; . . . yet I, Jahveh,
have been thy God from the land of Egypt, thou
knewest no God beside me ; nor was there any
Saviour beside me."

On the whole, the language of the prophets
compels us to believe in a constantly increasing
degradation of the nation. It would be impossible to find words to express more forcibly the
utter corruption of the northern tribes, and,
saddest sign of all, the shameless impurity of
the women, than the words that are used by
Amos and Hosea. We need not dwell upon
them ; it is enough to notice that in every case
the evil is traced directly to the debasing worship of the idols, which intercourse with Phœnicia had brought among them. " They left the

[1] xiii. 1, 2, 4.

commandments of the Lord their God, and
made them molten images, even two calves, and
made a grove, and worshipped all the host of
heaven and served Baal, . . . and they followed
vanity and became vain, and went after the
heathen that were round about them, concern-
ing whom the Lord had charged them that they
should not do like them. . . . . Therefore the
Lord was very angry with Israel, and removed
them out of His sight : there was none left but
the tribe of Judah only."

And Judah was drawn along the same fatal
path, by the same evil influences. We have
seen how Tyrian traders and Tyrian settlers
paved the way for the adoption of their national
religion. After the influence of one of their
own princesses had procured the erection of a
"grove," or rather an idolatrous symbol for
Ashtoreth, it was probably the Tyrian colony in
Jerusalem that supplied the most constant worshippers there, and Tyrian women that led the
Jews into a participation in its unholy rites. At
the very commencement of the kingdom of
Judah, the great internal struggle begins which
forms the principal element of interest throughout its subsequent history. On the one side

was the Temple with its unrivalled splendour and
glorious associations. Round it gathered the
Aaronic priesthood, who assume fresh importance with the concentration of the national life
in the southern kingdom. At a later date
their spiritual pride and formalism made them
the bitterest foes of the truly inspired prophets.
But at this time the priests and the prophets
were contending side by side for the honour of
Jahveh. Opposed to them was the party of the
court, led by one of those commanding and
resolute women that play so prominent a part
in Jewish history. Maachah, the granddaughter
of Absalom, seems to have been gifted with all
the fascinating beauty of David's favourite son,
and to have exercised an irresistible influence
over her husband Rehoboam and her son Abijah,
at whose court she retained the position of
queen-mother. And mainly by her influence
" Judah did evil in the sight of the Lord ; for
they built them high places and images and
groves on every high hill and under every
green tree ; and they did according to all the
abominations of the nations which the Lord cast
out before the children of Israel." We have
here all the usual phrases to denote a revival of

the worship of Ashtoreth ; and we are expressly told[1] that the darkest features of that worship were not wanting ; that the unhallowed consecration of men and women to the service of the goddess was practised. The corruption was checked for the time by the vigour of Asa, who destroyed the private sanctuary of Maachah, burnt the obscene image to which her worship was offered, and "her he removed from being queen." The victory was for the time with the priests and the prophets of the Lord. But the alliance with the northern kingdom, which brought prosperity to Jehoshaphat, was destined to have the most fatal effects upon his country. The good that he had done by carrying on the religious reaction of Asa, and adding to it a zeal for promoting among his people a knowledge of "the Book of the Law," was more than counterbalanced by the marriage of his son Jehoram with Athaliah, the daughter of Ahab and Jezebel. Even in her husband's reign she had succeeded in restoring the worship of

[1] 1 Kings xiv. 24.

[2] The word employed in 1 Kings xv. 13, and 2 Chron. xv. 16, means properly "fright," "horror," and was undoubtedly an Asherah. Cp. Dict. Bible, i., p. 849*a*, and Movers, i., p. 571.

Baal ; [1]—we can hardly suppose that it was then introduced for the first time, though we have not previously any explicit mention of it ; for it seems an inseparable concomitant of the worship of Ashtoreth. But her evil energies were roused to the utmost by the slaughter of her son Ahaziah by Jehu, and the subsequent massacre of the worshippers of Baal at Samaria. Successive calamities had almost exhausted the family of David, and now "when Athaliah saw that Ahaziah was dead, she arose and destroyed all the seed-royal." One alone escaped, and he but an infant. Then "the worship of Baal, uprooted by Jehu in Samaria, sprang up with renewed vigour in Jerusalem. The adherents of Baal, exiled from the northern kingdom, no doubt took refuge in the south. The temple became a quarry for the rival sanctuary. The stones and sacred vessels were employed to build or to adorn the temple of Baal, which rose, as it would seem, even within the temple precincts."[2] But the queen does not appear to have felt herself strong enough to crush the

---

[1] See 2 Chron. xxi. 11, 13.

[2] Stanley, ii., p. 394 ; 2 Kings xi. 18 ; 2 Chron. xxiii. 17, 18.

worship of Jahveh, which went on side by side with the rites of the pagan sanctuary.

No scene in the sacred history is more dramatic, and few more familiar, than that in which the chief priest Jehoiada overthrew the usurping idolatress, and restored at once the rightful heir and the true religion. The writer of the Book of Chronicles (probably himself a priest)[1] takes great delight in recording the zeal and gladness with which the house of God was restored, which "the sons of Athaliah, that wicked woman, had broken up," and the dedicated things of the house of the Lord replaced, which they had bestowed upon Baalim.[2] But soon the brightness was clouded over again. On the death of the aged Jehoiada, the king "hearkened unto the princes of Judah,"[3] who always appear as the leaders of the idolatrous party opposed to the priests and the prophets.

---

[1] See Milman's note (i., p. 328). The majority of commentators accept the constant tradition of the Jews, that the work was compiled by Ezra.

[2] 2 Chron. xxiv. 7.

[3] 2 Chron. xxiv. 17. Some part of the evil may have been due to the influence of the king's mother, Zibiah of Beersheba, a place noted at this time for its idolatry (Amos viii. 14).

It is natural that those who were brought most into contact with the Tyrian merchants, and who had been most deeply tainted by the corruptions of what was practically a Tyrian court under Athaliah, should be most zealous in the service of the Tyrian deities. "And they left the house of Jahveh, God of their fathers, and served Asherah and idols. Yet sent he prophets to them to bring them again unto Jahveh, and they testified against them; but they would not give ear."

With the death of Athaliah the direct influence of Tyre on Judah had ceased. But we cannot doubt that very much indirect influence still continued to be exerted, through the agencies to which we have often referred. An incidental expression in Isaiah (ii. 16) shows us that the commerce of Uzziah still loaded the ships of Tarshish with articles of costly and beautiful merchandize.[1] But his own name ("the help of Jahveh," or in the form Azariah, "the strength of Jahveh,") shows that he had not forsaken the national God. And the reference in the prophet of the time—Amos[2]—to the kidnapping incursions of the Tyrians, shows that

Stanley, ii., p. 435.   [2] i., 9.

there can have been no close alliance or friendship between the two nations. This is further
confirmed by the fact that his reign appears
to be a period of the great predominance of the
priesthood, and the increased magnificence of
the temple service. We may notice also that
Amos, though belonging to the southern kingdom, went into the land of Israel to deliver his
prophecies, and seems to have felt that there
was much less need for his indignant invectives
in the kingdom of Judah.

But the priests soon fell before the temptation
that everywhere besets the professors of a domi-
nant creed ; and a religion which had become
little better than a formal sham was unable to
hold its own against the seductions of a sensual
idolatry which appealed with so much force to
the vicious and luxurious nobles. The accession
of Ahaz marks the commencement of a new
period of declension. His father Jotham had done
that which was right in the sight of Jahveh,
though under his reign the people yet did cor-
ruptly, and offered incense in the high places
or consecrated mounds,[1] which might be sometimes even in valleys (Jer. xvii. 21) or in

[1] Cp. Movers, i., p. 675.

the streets of Jerusalem (2 Kings xvii. 9, Ezek. xvi. 31), and on which an irregular worship was offered, sometimes to Jahveh, at other times to heathen deities. But Ahaz "made molten images for Baalim, and burnt his children in the fire, after the abominations of the heathen whom Jahveh had cast out before the children of Israel. He sacrificed also and burnt incense in the high places, and on the hills, and under every green tree."[1] What is implied in the latter is shown but too plainly by the words of Hosea (iv. 13). These and similar phrases point to the influence of the old Canaan-itish and therefore Phœnician idolatry; but Ahaz personally seems to have been rather devoted to foreign religious practices, to the ritual of the gods of Damascus, and the wizard-ries of the remoter East.[2] His reign is one of the darkest passages in the history of Judah; it is succeeded by a brightness as of the Indian summer before the gloom of winter settles on the land, or the glory of the setting sun, that

---

[1] 2 Chron. xxviii. 2—4.

[2] Movers (i., pp. 65, 66) maintains that Ahaz adopted the purer Magian star-worship, as contrasted with the corrupt Phœnician cult. See above, p. 171.

after a day of clouds and storm illumines the
world for a transient while before it sinks into
the shades of night. At the stern rebuke of the
prophet Micah,[1] the king Hezekiah and the
nation were awakened to a sense of their sinful
apostasy. A vast sacrifice was offered in expia-
tion of the national guilt. " And Hezekiah spake
unto the heart[2] of all the Levites that taught
the good knowledge of the Lord, and they
did eat throughout the feast seven days,
offering peace offerings and making confes-
sion unto Jahveh, God of their fathers. . . .
So there was great joy in Jerusalem ; for since
the time of Solomon the son of David, king of
Israel, there was not the like in Jerusalem."
The " high places," that had formed so easy a
transition to pagan worship, and the brazen
serpent, that appeared to link the worship of
Jahveh on to one of the most widely extended
of heathen superstitions,[3] were alike destroyed ;
" the uprooting of those delightful shades, the
levelling of those consecrated altars, the destruc-

---

[1] The scene is graphically described in Stanley's Lectures, ii., pp. 463—465.

[2] So the Hebrew in 2 Chron. xxx. 22, 26.

[3] Cp. Cox, "Aryan Mythology," ii., p. 116.

tion of that mysterious figure, which Moses had made in the wilderness, must have been a severe shock to the religious feelings of the nation."[1] But they were one and all fatal lures to lead them into the unhallowed worship of Phœnicia,[2] and therefore the king destroyed them. The terrible reaction under his youthful son Manasseh is to be ascribed directly to the influence of the "party of the princes," and we cannot trace Phœnician influence in it, except so far as, according to a remark made above, the nobles were those peculiarly liable to be affected by the opinions and practices of wealthy foreign merchants. It is more just to say that the evil leaven, once introduced by the example of the Canaanites within the borders, and their powerful maritime kinsfolk, had never ceased to work among those classes, where it found its most congenial matter.

Once again the abominable rites of Astarte were practised even within the sacred precincts;[3] the houses of her devotees were hard by the house of the Lord, and in them the women wove

---

[1] Stanley, ii., p. 467.
[2] Cp. Movers, i., pp. 560—577.
[3] 2 Kings xxi. 5—7.

decorated hangings for the emblem under which she was worshipped. Now for the first time in Judah a terrible persecution was directed against the worshippers of Jahveh, and the voices of the prophets were silenced. The suicidal attempt was but too successful ; the after-reformation of Josiah, though carried out with an earnestness, a thoroughness, we may almost add a bitterness, to which we find no earlier parallel, came too late to root out the growing corruption of the nation. " Large as is the space occupied by it in the historical books, by the contemporary prophets it is never mentioned at all."[1] The national worship of Jahveh had been crushed out of the land, or had withered in the presence of more alluring idolatries ; but with its extinction the national life had been paralyzed at the heart ; the Jews had lost their *raison d'être* for independent national existence ; and the operation of the natural laws of history, which are indeed but the execution on earth of the judgments of God, rendered their captivity inevitable.

We have thus traced, rapidly and incompletely, but with details perhaps sufficient for

[1] Stanley, ii., p. 503.

our present purpose, the history of the lapse
into idolatry on the part of the children of
Israel. So far as it needs any other explanation than that which is furnished by the attraction of a sensuous faith and a licentious practice
upon the mass of mankind, this is supplied, we
believe, by the action of Phœnician influence
from without, strongly supported by the example of the incorporated Canaanites, and
sometimes roused into greater activity by special
political circumstances.

But here again the question presents itself to
us, Is there not another and a brighter side to
the picture ? Can we believe that the Shepherd
and Guide of His chosen people placed them in
a position where they would be exposed to the
strongest temptations, from which nothing but
evil could result?—that no rich blessing was
intended to the world by all these centuries of
trial and discipline? I think that several considerations may be found, to help us in seeing
this matter aright. In the first place, the nature
of the Phœnician religion was in itself a safe-
guard. Much more might have been said, perhaps in some places ought to have been said,
that has intentionally been passed over, about

the corrupting and degrading character of the worship and its votaries. But while these characteristics only enhanced its attractions among the masses, especially of the wealthy and luxurious, there must have been in every generation many pure and noble spirits to whom they caused invincible repugnance. We may say with reverence that it was of vital importance to the Divine scheme of the education of the race that a firm and *hereditary* belief in the One Living and True God should be maintained, at least in one selected people. We see from the religious history of Greece and Rome how impossible it was for any such belief to gain firm hold of the mind of a nation when supported only by the speculations of philosophers. Plato's Idea of the Beautiful, or the Stoic's pantheistic conception of the all-pervading world-spirit, was an utterly inadequate substitute for "the Lord God of our fathers" of the Israelite. But let us conceive, if we can, of Athens standing to the kingdom of Israel in the relation that Tyre actually occupied. Let us fancy the brutal worship of Baal-Moloch, the wild orgies of Ashtoreth, replaced by hymns to Apollo, the glorious god of light, such as that chanted as

his morning pæan by Ion;[1] by the praises that
Cleanthes taught his countrymen to offer to
Zeus, "the almighty one from everlasting, of
whom we are the offspring;" and by the Homeric
stories of Athena, the ever-maiden goddess of
wisdom, helper of heroes in fair and noble deeds
of daring. Can we not readily believe that under
the charms of a mythology such as this, not
only the lowest, but even the highest spirits of
the nation, might have been led astray from the
faith of their fathers? And when the process
of decay, of misconception, of fouler aftergrowth
of legend had begun, where would then have
been the spring of living water which, choked
for a while, and all but hidden among the
Jews, had never been entirely dried, but which
when the appointed time had come, and its
fountains were unsealed and purified by the
Incarnate Lord, broke forth once more for the
healing of the nations?

Again, we must remember that the part which
a nation plays in the development of the great
world's life, depends far more upon the height
to which its most exalted spirits rise, than upon
the depths to which the mass of its members

---

[1] Cp. Eur. Ion, 82—153.

sometimes sink. It matters very little to us now, except as a warning (and such are sadly plentiful), that the princes of Judah in the days of Manasseh gave themselves up to work all manner of evil; but the Church throughout all time has been and will be unspeakably the richer for the visions that in the darkness, and surely also through the darkness, were given to the aged prophet. Phœnicia and Canaan, Baal and Ashtoreth, had done their worst, and with terrible success, to blind the eyes of the bulk of the nation to truth and goodness, when the Spirit of the Lord spoke in the words of Isaiah the promises that have been the stay of His people ever since.

The Aryan nations, as M. Pictet well expresses it,[1] in presence, not of error, but only of nature, held their primitive monotheism but loosely, and under the influence of a language of boundless fertility, that lent itself readily to the development of myths, this soon was changed in every instance into a constantly degenerating polytheism. But the storms of fierce temptation that assailed the Hebrews on every side acted on their faith, as the national discipline

[1] Les Origines Indo-Européennes, ii., p. 710.

acted on the children of Sparta : the feeble and sickly perished, but those who endured to the end were made into models of healthful and vigorous manhood. Monotheism among the Jews attained to a strength of grasp upon the national conscience, a depth of sure conviction that is only given to truth that has wrestled in a long stern struggle with error. " A fugitive and cloistered virtue, unexercised and unbreathed, that never sallies out and sees her adversary, but slinks out of the race, where that immortal garland is to be run for, not without dust and heat," will never work any great deliverance, be it in man or in nation. " That virtue which is but a youngling in the contemplation of evil, and knows not the utmost that vice promises to her followers, and rejects it, is but a blank virtue, not a pure ; her whiteness is but an excremental whiteness." [1] The faith of the later Hebrews in the Unity of the Godhead was no mere product of " a religious instinct," no fragile fancy of prophet or poet :—

> But iron dug from central gloom,
> And heated hot with burning fears,
> And dipt in baths of hissing tears,

[1] Milton, " Areopagitica."

And battered with the shocks of doom,
To shape and use.

And if, as Mr. Gladstone has nobly said, " the history of the race of Adam before the Advent is the history of a long and varied but incessant preparation for the Advent," we cannot fail to recognize in the powerful influence of Phœnicia on the eastern as well as the western world one great element in that preparation. Here too the eye of faith will recognize one of the "diverse parts and diverse manners" in which a wisdom, sometimes far beyond our ken, but always in its own good way, was laying deep and sure the foundations of the Everlasting City of God.

FINIS.

Printed by Watson and Hazell, London and Aylesbury.

BY THE SAME AUTHOR.

Our National Universities. In 8vo, price 1s.

LONDON: HODDER AND STOUGHTON.

Second Edition. Crown 8vo, price 3s. 6d., cloth.

The Light of the World: an Essay on the Distinctive Features of Christian as compared with Pagan Ethics.

CRITICAL NOTICES.

" It would be difficult to praise too highly the spirit, the burden, the conclusions, or the scholarly finish of this beautiful essay. There are abundant signs of ripe scholarship, rich culture, and the modesty of extensive knowledge. We accept the volume with singular satisfaction, as a very valuable contribution to Christian Ethics."—*British Quarterly Review.*

" We are not late in paying our tribute to this little volume : it might seem so, from the announcement of the second edition, but in fact the essay has rapidly become popular, and placed itself beyond the necessity of any introduction on our part. It deserves its success. Mr. Wilkins has not only produced the Hulsean Dissertation of the year : he has also written the best essay we have upon his subject. . . . The essay is beautifully written, abounds with the mosaic work of apt quotation from an unusual breadth of reading, and is as remarkable for reverence as for pure taste in other respects."—*London Quarterly Review.*

" A clever and very readable essay. The range, at once, of reading and thought which it exhibits is very striking."—*Literary Churchman.*

" It is not surprising that this most scholarly treatise should have gained the Hulsean Prize, or that it should have rapidly passed into a second edition. It cannot fail to be read with the greatest interest by all students."—*Watchman.*

Fp. 8vo, price 3s. 6d., cloth.

The Orations of Cicero against Catilina, with Notes and an Introduction. Translated from the German of Karl Halm, with many additions.

" The best school-book, we think, that has ever come under our notice. The excellence of the original is sufficiently guaranteed, by its appearing in Haupt and Sauppe's series, and its practical usefulness fully established by the sale of seven editions in the course of a few years. But we do not hesitate to affirm that the English edition is rendered far superior to the original by the extensive additions of Professor Wilkins, which bear ample testimony, not simply to his varied critical and literary acquirements, but also to the correctness of his judgment respecting the difficulties and wants of the generality of students. There is scarcely a note in the original to which important additions have not been made by the editor."—*British Quarterly Review.*

" This very handy little edition of the Catiline orations is based on the German edition of Halm, to which Mr. Wilkins has added a good many notes of his own, all useful. Most of these additional notes bear on philology ; many, however, explain Roman customs and phrases, and there are also frequent parallel examples of Ciceronian usages which are especially useful to a student beginning to make acquaintance with the author. Indeed we have never seen a book which we should feel more inclined to put into the hands of a boy as a first introduction to the great orator."—*Athenæum.*

LONDON: MACMILLAN AND CO.

SECOND EDITION.

In crown 8vo, price 7s. 6d., cloth.

MODERN SCEPTICISM.

A COURSE OF LECTURES

Delivered at the Request of the Christian Evidence Society.

With an Explanatory Paper by the Right Rev. C. J. ELLICOTT, D.D., Lord Bishop of Gloucester and Bristol.

CONTENTS.

*** The above Lectures, and the Bishop of Gloucester's Paper, may also be had separately, price 6d. each.

London: HODDER & STOUGHTON, 27, Paternoster Row.

WORKS BY THE LATE DEAN ALFORD.

1. Truth and Trust : Lessons of the War. By the
late HENRY ALFORD, D.D., Dean of Canterbury. His
Last Work. Fcap. 8vo, 2s. 6d.

2. The State of the Blessed Dead. New
Edition. Square 16mo, 1s. 6d.

3. The Coming of the Bridegroom. New
Edition. Square 16mo, 1s. 6d., cloth.

Cues from all Quarters ; or, Literary Musings
of a Clerical Recluse. In crown 8vo, 7s. 6d., cloth.

A Second Series of "Ecclesia :" Church
Problems Considered, in a Series of Essays. Edited by
H. R. REYNOLDS, D.D. List of Writers : Revs. W. Lind-
say Alexander, D.D.; Henry Batchelor; R. W. Dale,
M.A.; Enoch Mellor, A.M., D.D.; H. R. Reynolds, D.D.
Prof. Wilkins; and Josiah Gilbert, Esq. 8vo, 8s. 6d.

Bible Music. Being Variations in Many Keys
on Musical Themes from Scripture. By Rev. FRANCIS
JACOX, B.A. In Crown 8vo, price 6s., cloth.

BY THE SAME AUTHOR.

Secular Annotations on Scripture
Texts. Crown 8vo, 6s.

SPECTATOR.—" By 'Secular Annotations' Mr. Jacox means illustrations
from what is commonly called profane history and literature. . . A singularly
interesting volume. The work of a man of wide reading."

Second Series of Secular Annotations
on Scripture Texts. Crown 8vo, 6s.

The Life and Times of the Rev. John
WESLEY, M.A., Founder of the Methodists. By the
Rev. LUKE TYERMAN. Author of " The Life of the Rev.
Samuel Wesley," etc. With three Portraits. In 3 vols.,
8vo, price 12s. each.

FREEMAN.—"The best biography of the great leader of modern active
Christianity." EVANGELICAL MAGAZINE. — " Mr. Tyerman's work will
henceforth be regarded as the standard life of Wesley." CHRISTIAN WORK.
—" By far the fullest and most complete life that has been written."

London: HODDER & STOUGHTON, 27, Paternoster Row.

Lightning Source UK Ltd.
Milton Keynes UK
UKHW022058090522
402738UK00003B/283

9 781358 058486